FM 10-16
(TM 4-42.21)

GENERAL FABRIC REPAIR

JULY, 2013

TABLE OF CONTENTS

iii

EDITOR'S NOTE

This volume contains the July, 2013 version of US Army Field Manual 10-16 – General Fabric Repair. I first started using this manual as a private when I was too cheap/broke to take damaged uniforms and equipment to the tailor shop for repair. I had and still have a much older copy of this manual that my platoon sergeant gave me long ago after he ripped me up for having an unserviceable piece of gear. I won't see this manual contains everything you need to know about how to sew. It does however, contain everything even the dumbest person needs to know to be able to effectively repair damaged gear and make it serviceable if not exactly pretty.

I have modified this copy somewhat by simplifying the table of contents and I have omitted the large list of figures and tables from the chapter of contents. Just about every description has an accompanying illustration or illustrations to go with it and almost every section has a table or two. As with all the other US Army manuals I am making available as hardcopies I have also renumbered the pages to be consecutive throughout the book instead of the weird chapter numbering system the military uses and that I always hated. I have attempted to fix all page references to reflect the new numbering but it id entirely possible that I have missed one or more.

My goal in compiling these was to make them available at an affordable price using modern Print-On-Demand (POD) technology. I hope these manuals are instructive.

If you discover any typos or incorrect references please send an email to info@military-history.us with the mistake and which page it is on so I can fix it in subsequent releases.

TM 4-42.21 (FM 10-16)
General Fabric Repair
July 2013

DISTRIBUTION RESTRICTION. Approved for public release; distribution is unlimited

Headquarters Department of the Army

Publication of TM 4-42.21, 24 July 2013, supersedes FM 10-16, General Fabric Repair, and 24 May 2000.

This special conversion to the TM publishing medium/nomenclature has been accomplished to comply with TRADOC doctrine restructuring requirements. The title and content of TM 4-42.21 is identical to that of the superseded FM 10-16.

This special conversion does not integrate any changes in Army doctrine since 24 May 2000 and does not alter the publication's original references; therefore, some sources cited in this TM may no longer be current. For the status of official Department of the Army (DA) publications, consult DA Pam 25-30, Consolidated Index of Army Publications, and Blank Forms, at http://armypubs.army.mil/2530.html. DA Pam 25-30 is updated as new and revised publications, as well as changes to publications are published. For the content/availability of specific subject matter, contact the appropriate proponent.

PREFACE

This technical manual is a guide for fabric repair specialists, personnel qualified in MOS 92S, grades E1 through E7. It can be used by personnel in both mobile and fixed repair units. This manual consists of general instructions for the inspection and repair of military clothing, textiles, canvas, and webbing. It covers methods for sewing by hand and by machine. It includes directions for different kinds of stitches, seams, darns, and patches. It explains how to replace fasteners (zippers) and hardware items.

Publications which pertain to fabric repair are listed at the back of the manual.

This publication applies to the Active Army, the Army National Guard (ARNG), /Army National Guard of the United States (ARNGUS), and the United States Army Reserve (USAR) unless otherwise stated. The proponent of this publication is HQ TRADOC. Send comments and recommendations on DA Form 2028 (Recommended Changes to Publications and Blank Forms) directly to:

Training Directorate
Quartermaster Training Division
ATTN ATCL AQ
401 1ST STREET
FORT LEE, VIRGINIA 23801-1511

Unless this publication states otherwise, masculine nouns and pronouns do not refer exclusively to men.

CHAPTER 1 - INSPECTING AND MARKING CLOTHING AND TEXTILE ITEMS

SECTION I – Initial Inspections

1-1. When damaged clothing and textile items are received in a fabric repair shop, they are inspected. These inspections determine if the pieces of clothing and equipment can be economically repaired in the shop and then reissued. The individual items are classified by condition. Faded clothing, noticeably stained items and defective items which cannot be repaired or are not worth repairing are set aside. These items are used for scrap or for duties that damage clothing, such as painting. Items to be mended are marked with white or yellow tailors clay chalk. See Figure 1-1 for the symbol and meaning of each mark used during the inspection of clothing and textile items. Table 1-1 lists the areas marked by the initial inspector.

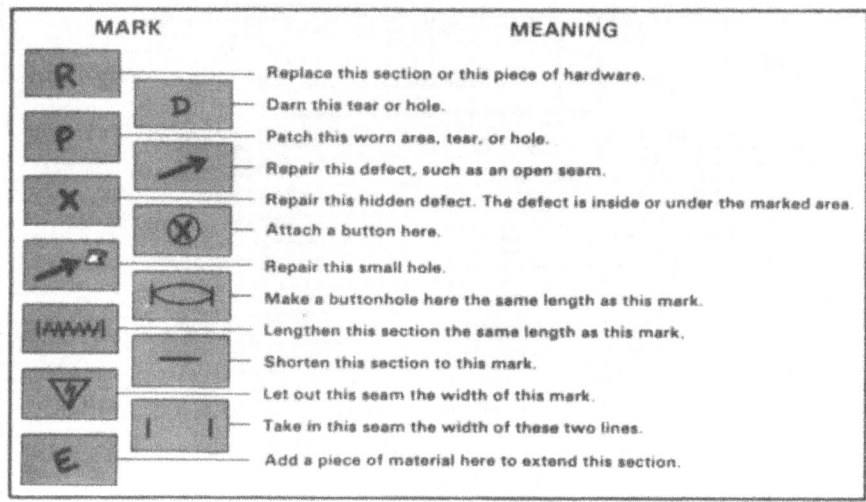

Figure 1-1. Chalk marks used on clothing and textile items

Defect	Repair
Worn fabric, especially in knee, crotch, seat, elbow, and underarm areas	Patch
Frayed edges, especially on hems, cuffs, collars, fly fronts and pocket flaps	Darn or patch
Holes	Patch
Rips and tears	Darn or patch
Open seams, broken stitching, and missing bar tacks	Restitch
Worn, torn, or missing tabs, straps, loops, and epaulets	Replace
Worn or damaged pockets and pocket flaps	Replace
Worn or torn linings	Darn, patch, or replace
Missing padding	Replace padding and restitch
Loose buttons and snaps	Restitch and replace missing or broken buttons and snaps
Frayed, enlarged, or ripped buttonholes	Remake
Broken zippers	Replace
Loose zippers	Restitch
Loose hook and pile fastener tape	Restitch
Missing hook and pile fastener tape	Replace
Missing or damaged buckles	Replace
Missing or worn drawstrings, laces, and belts	Replace
Missing or worn elastic	Replace
Other missing or defective fasteners or hardware	Replace
Areas that need alterations	Resize

Table 1-1. Areas marked in initial inspection of clothing and textiles

SECTION II – Final Inspections

1-2. After repairs are completed, pieces of clothing and textile items are inspected again. Each item is carefully examined to make sure all repairs were done and that no defects were overlooked. The quality of repair work is also checked during this inspection. Each repair is examined to make sure the correct size and color thread, type, and length of stitch, and type of seam were used. Breaks in stitching are checked to be sure they were tacked. Patches are inspected to be sure that they were installed correctly and that they match the color, texture, and weight of the fabric. Replaced parts such as zippers, snaps, and buttons are examined to make sure that the correct type and sizes were used and that they were attached correctly. Each item is also checked to make sure that a fabric repair specialist has not sewn together two pieces of fabric that should not have been joined. Items that pass inspection are reissued. Items that do not pass inspection are marked and returned to a fabric repair specialist for corrections.

CHAPTER 2 - HAND SEWING ON CLOTHING AND TEXTILES

SECTION I – Hand Sewing

2-1. Hand sewing is stitching done manually with a needle and thread. It is used when very fine or delicate work is necessary. For all other work, machine sewing is used as much as possible. Sewing by hand is done only when the item is too small or too large to repair by machine, or when the area to be repaired will not fit under the machine needle or presser foot.

SECTION II – Tools

2-2. The tools needed for hand sewing are few and simple. They are all shown in Figure 2-1 and described below.

Shears or Craftsman's Knife

2-3. Shears (1) are used to cut the fabric and thread. Their handles are also used to put a crease in a piece of fabric. Sharpen the points and edges regularly to make cutting easier and more accurate. Lubricate the screw when necessary and wipe the shears clean. Do not use shears to cut anything heavier than fabric, because it will dull the blades. Craftsman's knives (2) are used to rip out stitching and to pen or lengthen buttonholes. Tighten the blades when they are loose. Replace the blades when they become dull

Pins, Needles, & Thimbles

2-4. Straight pins (3) are used to hold two or more layers of fabric together during sewing. Needles (3) are used to pierce fabric and to pull thread through cloth to make stitches. Needles come in various sizes. Some may have longer eyes. Use only clean, sharp needles and pins. A thimble (3) is a metal cap which is placed over the middle finger of the sewing hand to protect the finger and to make it easier to push the needle through heavy material or several layers of fabric. Although a thimble is awkward to wear, its use is encouraged to prevent injuries.

Thread

2-5. Thread (4) is used to sew two or more layers of cloth together. It may consist of a single strand called a ply or several strands which have been twisted together to make a stronger thread (Figure 2-2, page 14). A two-ply thread consists of two strands; a three-ply thread consists of three strands, and so on. Thread is made of cotton, nylon, or polyester. It comes in various colors and weights. To mend an item, use the same color and type of thread that was used to make the item.

Ruler or Measuring Tape

2-6. A ruler or measuring tape (5) is used to gage accurately the length and width of seams and hems.

Tailor's Clay Chalk

2-7. During inspections, yellow or white tailor's clay chalk (6) is used to mark defects. During sewing operations, it is used to mark seam-stitching and hem-stitching guidelines on cloth.

1. SHEARS

2. CRAFTSMAN'S KNIFE

3. PINS, NEEDLES, AND THIMBLE

4. THREAD

5. MEASURING TAPE

6. TAILOR'S CLAY CHALK

7. IRON

8. BUTTONHOLE CUTTER

Figure 2-1. Sewing tools

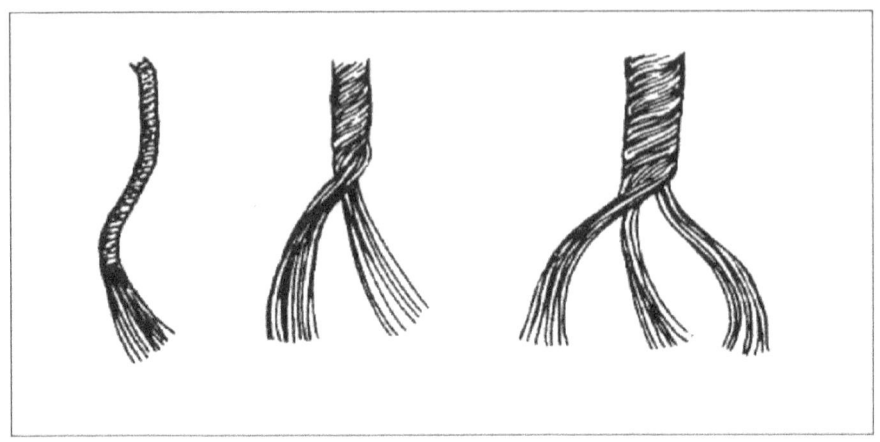

Figure 2-2. Singly-ply, two-ply, and three-ply thread

Iron

2-8. An iron (7) is used to press open seams and press down folds to make sewing easier.

Buttonhole Cutter

2-9. A buttonhole cutter (8) is a hand-held device used to cut slits in cloth for buttonholes.

SECTION III – Preparation of Needle & Thread

2-10. Threading a needle and making a knot in the thread (Figure 2-3) takes nimble fingers and good eyesight. It gets easier with practice. Procedures to thread a needle and make a knot are described below.

- Using shears; cut a piece of thread about 36 inches long from a spool. Do not attempt to break the thread manually or to bite through it. This frays the end and makes it more difficult to get the thread through the eye of the needle. Do not cut a piece of thread any longer than 1 yard. Thread that is too long tangles and knots.
- Hold the needle in one hand, and grasp the thread about 1/2 inch from the end. To see the eye more easily, hold the needle up to light or against a light background. Stick the end of the thread through the eye of the needle.
- If sewing with a single thread, feed or pull 5 or 6 inches of thread through the eye, and knot the other end. If sewing with a double thread, pull one end of the thread through the eye until both ends are even, and then knot the ends together.
- To make a knot, first make a loop by wrapping the end of the thread once around the tip of the forefinger. Slide this loop off the fingertip with the thumb, and pass the end of the thread through the loop. Grasp the end of the thread, and pull the knot taut to set

it. To make a larger knot, repeat this step and adjust the thread so that the second knot lands on the first one

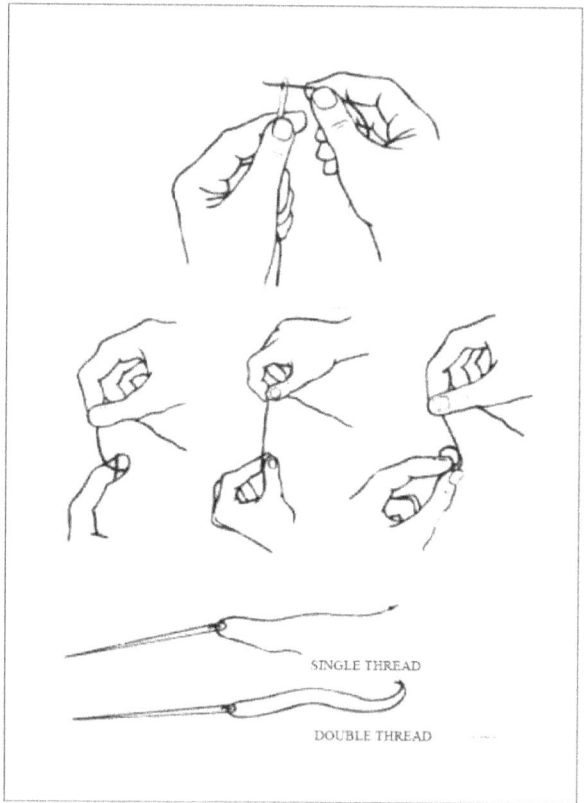

SINGLE THREAD

DOUBLE THREAD

Figure 2-3. Threading a needle and making a knot

SECTION IV – Hand Stitches

2-11. There are dozens of stitches that can be sewn by hand. A variety of hand stitches are used to mend military clothing and textile items.

Basting Stitch

2-12. The basting stitch (Figure 2-4) is very common in tailoring. Before any permanent stitches are put into a garment, a temporary stitch is put in to hold the material in position or to see if the garments will fit the individual properly. To make a row of basting stitches

- Thread the needle with a contrasting color of thread so the stitches will be easier to see and remove later.
- Stick the needle through the cloth, and pull the thread through the cloth to the knot.
- Stick the needle into the cloth and weave the needle in and out of the cloth several times. Stitch alongside, instead of directly on, the

line where the permanent stitches will be sewn. Make the stitches two or three times longer than running stitches.

- Pick up as many stitches as possible before pulling the needle and thread through the cloth. Continue to stitch to the end of the row.
- Make a knot in the thread close to the cloth and cut off the remaining thread.
- After the permanent stitch has been placed into the material, the basting stitch is then removed.
- The length of the basting stitch depends on the work that has to be performed. If the stitch is placed on the collar of a jacket, many stitches are needed to hold the material in place, but on the legs of trousers when they are being hemmed, only a few are needed and they can be placed a reasonable distance apart.

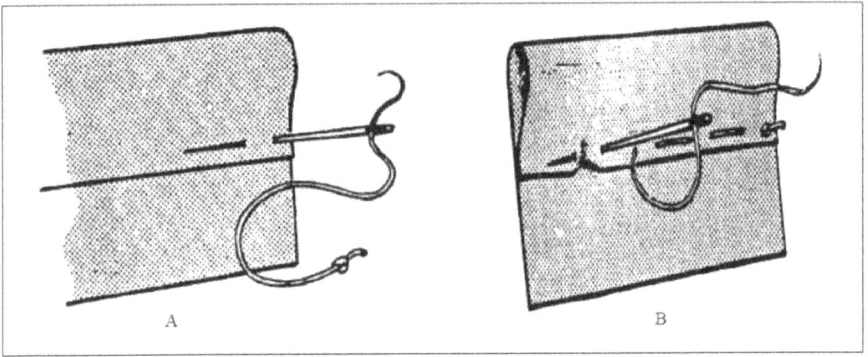

Figure 2-4. Basting stitch

Felling Stitch (Vertical Hemming) or Overhand Stitch

2-13. The felling stitch (Figure 2-5) is a form of blind stitch used in most instances to hem or to hold two pieces of material together where a machine cannot satisfactorily operate, for example, sleeves on wool jackets. It is possible to sew the lining by machine; however, the machine sewn stitch through the sleeve would not present a neat military appearance. In some cases, the waistbands on trousers are felled in by hand. The felling stitch can be used only on smooth edges where no thread has become unraveled. The rough edges of the fabric are turned under before stitching. The length of the felling stitch is determined by the job it has to perform; normally, the felling stitches should be ⅛ of an inch apart, depending on the type of work to be done.

16

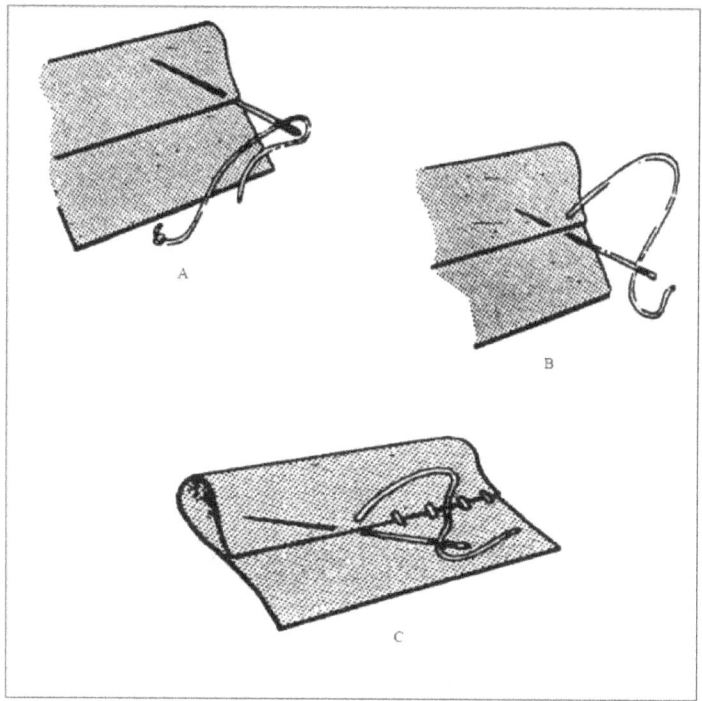

Figure 2-5. Felling stitch

Cross Stitch (Catch Stitch)

2-14. The cross stitch (Figure 2-6) is used to sew raw edges of material to keep it from raveling, as in hems. Cross stitches are blind stitches used in most instances to hem trouser legs and places where a blind stitch is necessary and a machine cannot satisfactorily operate. Cross stitches should be smooth, even, and completely hidden on the right side of the material. To make a row of cross stitches—

- Stick the needle through the cloth and pull the thread through the cloth to the knot.
- Backstitch to tack the row at the beginning. —
- Make a long diagonal stitch across the raw edge of the hem and stick the needle into the fabric of the garment. Securely catch the fabric but do not penetrate it completely.
- Take a small horizontal stitch back in the fabric of the garment.
- Make a long diagonal stitch across the raw edge of the hem so that the thread crosses over itself and stick the needle into the fabric of the hem. Penetrate the fabric of the hem completely but do not catch the underlying fabric of the garment with this stitch.
- Take a small horizontal stitch back in the fabric of the hem.

17

- Work diagonally back and forth across the raw edge, taking small horizontal stitches first on one side and then on the other. The finished row of stitches looks like interlocked X's. No stitches can be seen from the outside of the garment.
- Backstitch to tack the row at the end.
- Make a knot in the thread close to the cloth and cut off the remaining thread.

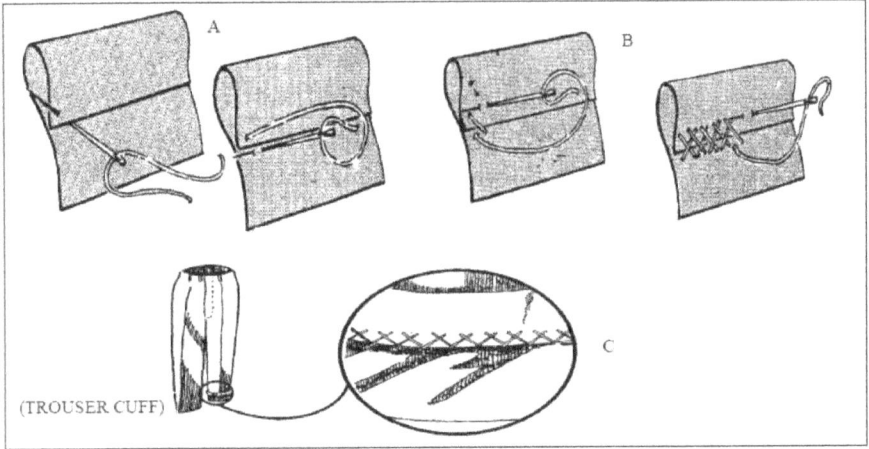

Figure 2-6. Cross stitch

Stoating Stitch

2-15. The stoating stitch (Figure 2-7) is used to repair a clean-edge or cut or tear in thick fabric. The stitches do not penetrate the fabric completely, so the repair does not show on the right side. To make a row of stoating stitches—

- Turn the fabric so that the wrong side is up and stick the needle into the thickness of the fabric ¼ inch from the end of the tear.
- Backstitch to tack the row at the beginning. Do not penetrate the cloth completely.
- Make a vertical stitch, coming up 1/16 inch away from the bottom edge of the tear. Do not penetrate the fabric.
- Working diagonally, stitch the needle into the fabric 1/16 inch away from the top edge of the tear.
- Continue to pass the needle over the tear diagonally and down through the tear vertically. Draw up all stitches firmly.
- Stop ¼ inch beyond the end of the tear.
- Backstitch to tack the row at the end.
- Make a knot in the thread close to the cloth, and cut off the remaining thread.

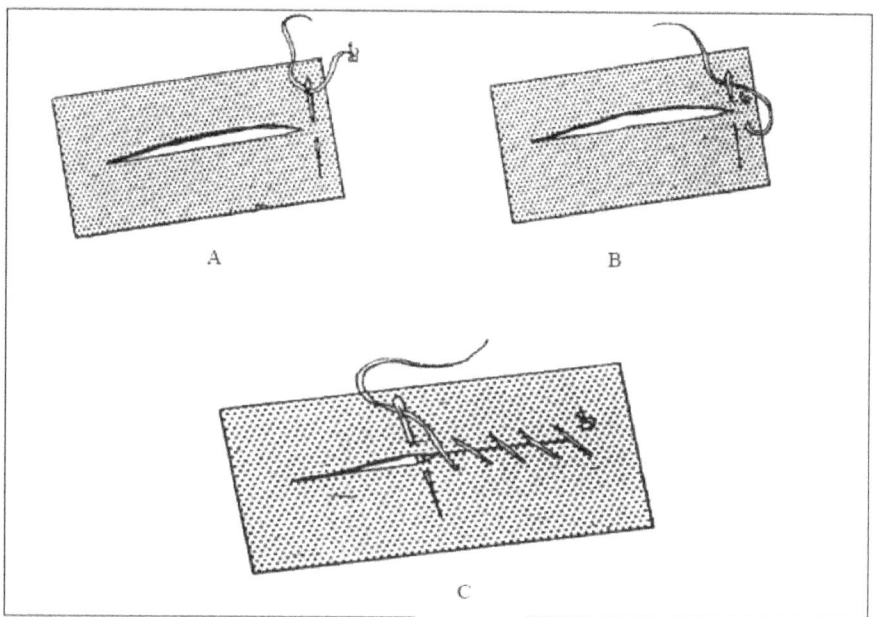

Figure 2-7. Stoating stitch

Whipstitch (Slant Hemming or Overcast Stitch)

2-16. The whipstitch (Figure 2-8) is used to finish raw edges to keep them from unraveling. To make a row of whipstitches—

- Stitch the needle through the cloth and pull the thread through the cloth to the knot.
- Backstitch to tack the beginning of the row.
- Stick the needle into the cloth 1/6 to ⅛ inch from the raw edge.
- Working diagonally; pass the thread and needle over the raw edge.
- Stick the needle into the cloth 1/16 to ⅛ inch from the raw edge and 1/16 to ⅛ inch from the previous stitch.
- Keep the stitches small and even and stitch until the raw edge is finished.
- Backstitch to tack the row at the end.
- Make a knot in the thread close to the cloth and cut off the remaining thread.

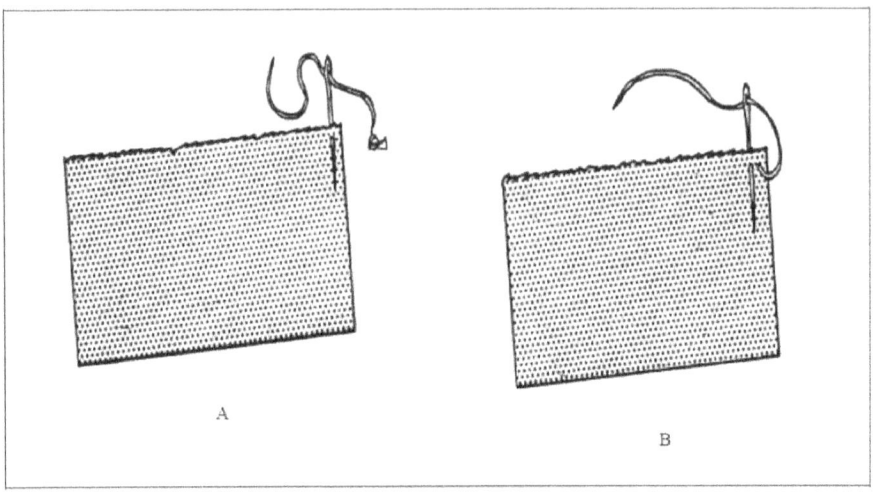

Figure 2-8. Whipstitch

Buttonhole Stitch

2-17. The buttonhole stitch (Figure 2-9) is used to finish and reinforce the raw edges of buttonholes and eyelets. To make a row of buttonhole stitches—

- Stick the needle up through the cloth 1/16 to ⅛ inch away from on edge of the buttonhole.
- Loop the thread in a circle.
- Stick the tip of the needle down through the circle and through the slash of the buttonhole.
- Stick the tip of the needle up through the cloth as close as possible to the last point where the needle came up. At the same time, take care to bring the needle up through the circle of thread.
- Draw up the needle and thread carefully so that a purl (a small, tight loop) forms on the edge of the slash.
- Repeat the stitch around the outside of the buttonhole. Keep the stitches close and even. Keep the purl on the edge of the slash.

Note: *See page 51, paragraph 4-23, for more on buttonholes.*

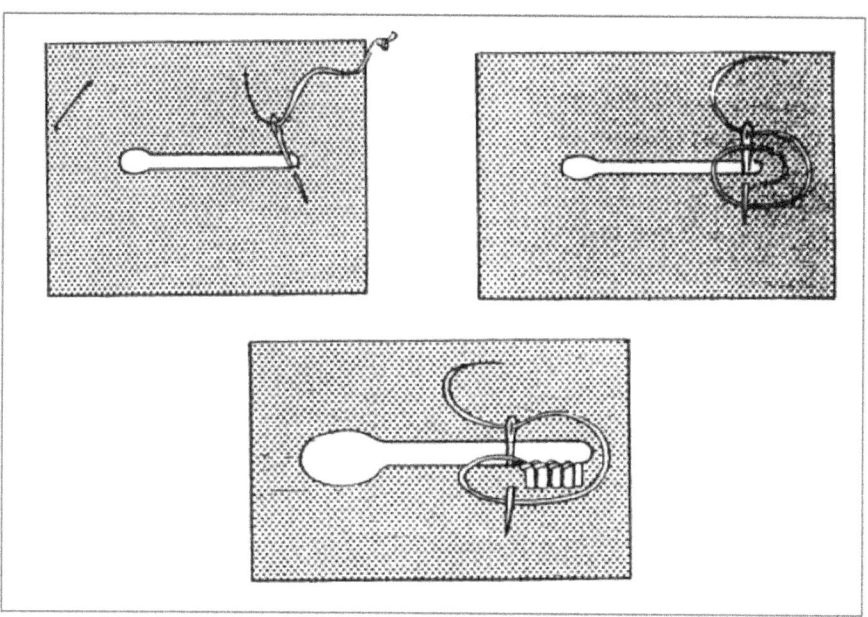

Figure 2-9. Buttonhole stitch

CHAPTER 3 – MACHINE SEWING ON CLOTHING AND TEXTILES

SECTION I – Machine Sewing

3-1. Machine sewing is stitching done on electrically powered equipment. Sewing machines form a stitch by interlocking a top thread and a bottom thread. The stitches made by sewing machines are more durable and more uniform in size and they look more tailored than stitches made by hand. Machine sewing is faster than hand sewing. For these reasons, machine sewing is used instead of hand sewing when possible.

SECTION II – Sewing Machines

3-2. The military uses several kinds of sewing machines. They include light-, medium-, and heavy-duty sewing machines, darning machines, and button-sewing machines (Figure 3-1). The kind of machine to use is determined by the weight of the fabric and the type of repair needed. Instructions for operating and maintaining sewing machines can be found in the appropriate technical manuals. Some information on needles, thread, stitch length, pressure, and tension is included here because they affect the appearance of the seam.

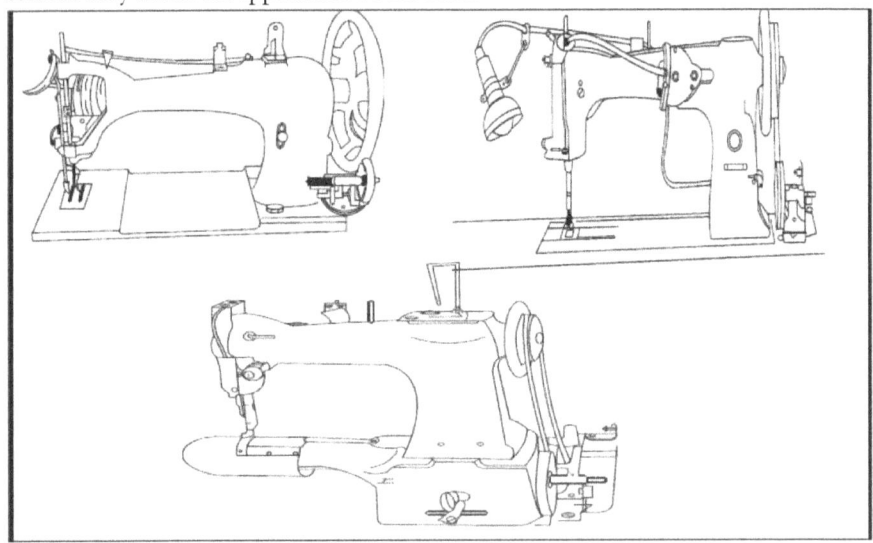

Figure 3-1. Typical Sewing Machines

Needles

3-3. Sewing machine needles (Figure 3-2) come in several types and sizes. The needles are classified by the type of shank, the type of point, and the length of the needle. Each type of sewing machine uses a different type of needle. Always use the correct type of needle, and replace bent or dull needles so that the machine operates properly. Needles come in numbered sizes. Needles with high numbers have bigger eyes and thicker shanks than needles with low numbers. The size needle to use is determined by the size thread needed to make the repair. Always match the size of the needle to the size of the thread so that the thread will pass easily through the eye.

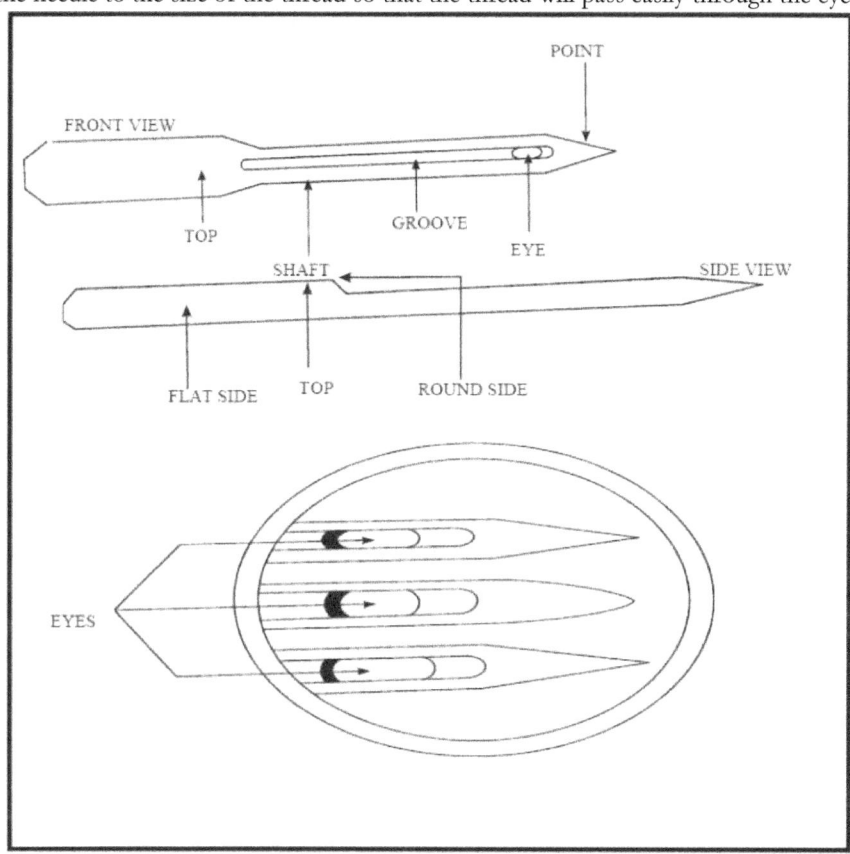

Figure 3-2. Sewing Machine Needles

Thread

3-4. Thread comes in several plies, weights, and colors. It is made of various materials, such as cotton, silk, or polyester. Thread also comes in two different twists. The twist is determined by the direction in which the fibers are spun together or the direction in which the plies are twisted together (Figure 3-3). Always use left-twist thread for the top thread, which is fed through the needle. Use left- or right-twist thread for the bottom thread, which is fed from the bobbin. Follow the directions in the appropriate technical manual to thread the needle and to wind the bobbin in each sewing machine. Machine Sewing on Clothing and Textiles

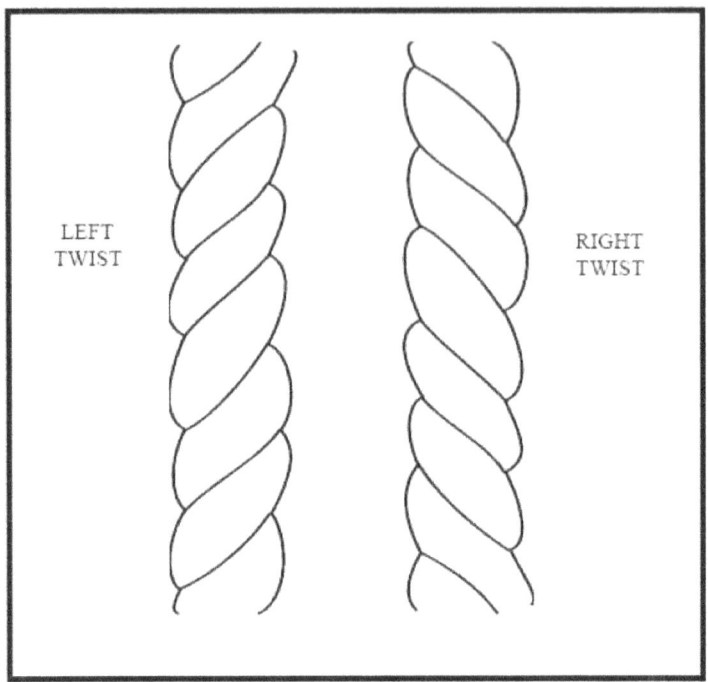

LEFT
TWIST

RIGHT
TWIST

Figure 3-3. Thread Twists

Stitch Length

3-5. The sewing machines used by the military make only one kind of stitch, a lockstitch (Figure 3-4). This stitch is formed when a top thread and a bottom thread interlock. The length of the stitch is determined by the forward movement of the cloth. The cloth is moved by feed dogs. The more fabric the feed dogs move forward with each stitch, the longer the stitches are. Stitch length is measured by the number of stitches per inch (Figure 3-5). Generally, short stitches are used on light fabrics. Long stitches are used on heavy fabric. Long stitches are also used for machine basting. Use the same stitch length to repair an item as that used to make it. Follow directions in the appropriate technical manual to change the stitch length on each sewing machine.

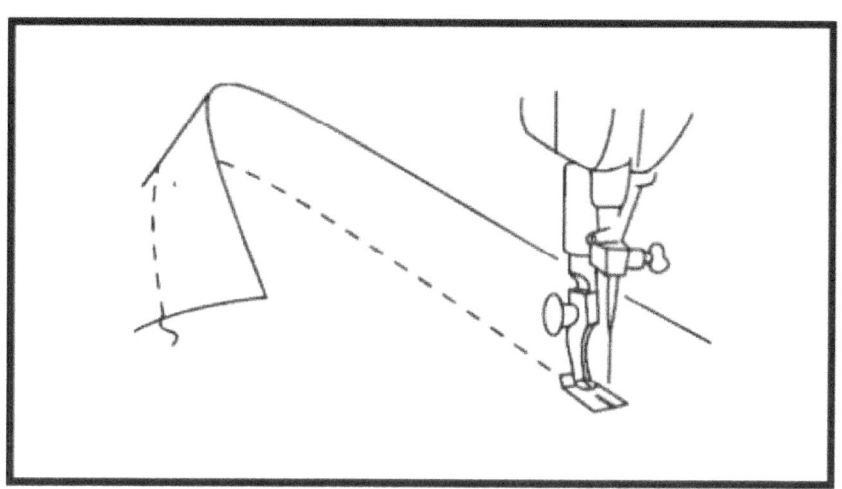

Figure 3-4. Lockstitch

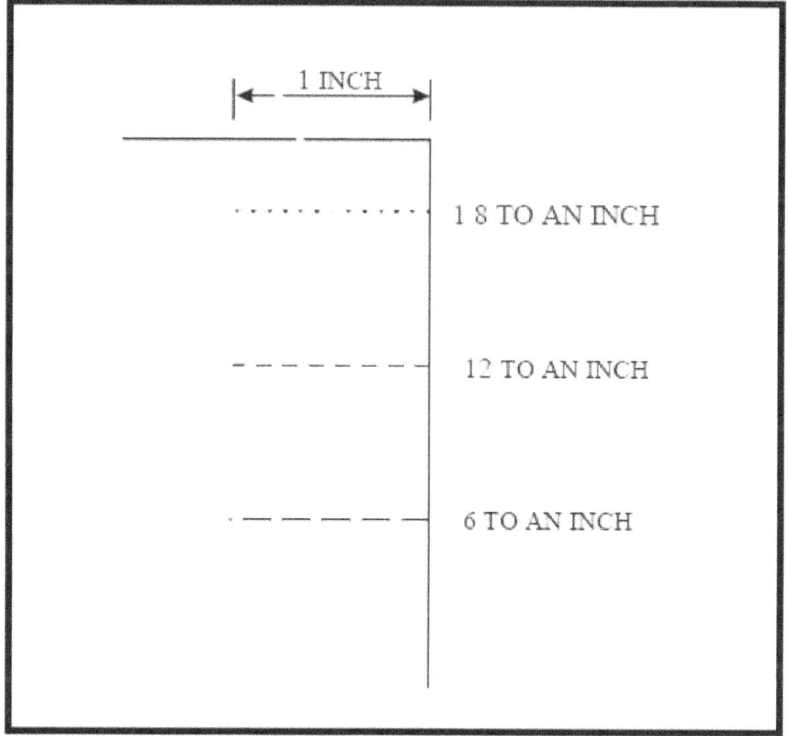

Figure 3-5. Stitch Length

Pressure

3-6. Pressure is the amount of force exerted downward on cloth by the presser foot. The presser foot holds the fabric in place while a stitch is being sewn.

The pressure and feed dogs then work together to move the fabric forward to the next stitch. If the pressure is too light, the feed dogs move the fabric forward unevenly. The amount of pressure needed depends on the weight of the cloth. As a rule, the lighter the fabric the less pressure needed to move it. Before sewing on fabric whose weight differs from that of the fabric last sewn on the machine, test the pressure by sewing a seam on scrap material. Use the same type of fabric and the same number of layers that will be used in the repair. If one layer of fabric slips, if stitches are skipped, or if the fabric is pulled down in the bobbin area, adjust the pressure. Follow directions in the appropriate technical manual to adjust the pressure on each sewing machine.

Tension

3-7. Tension is the amount of stress put on a thread. When the tension between the top thread and the bottom thread is correct and balanced, the connecting link of each lockstitch is in the center (Figure 3-6). The stitches look the same on both sides. When there is too much tension on the top thread or too little on the bottom thread, the link is on the bottom. When there is too much tension on both threads; the fabric puckers and the stitches break. When there is too little tension on both threads, the stitches have too much play, the threads form loops, and the seam is weak.

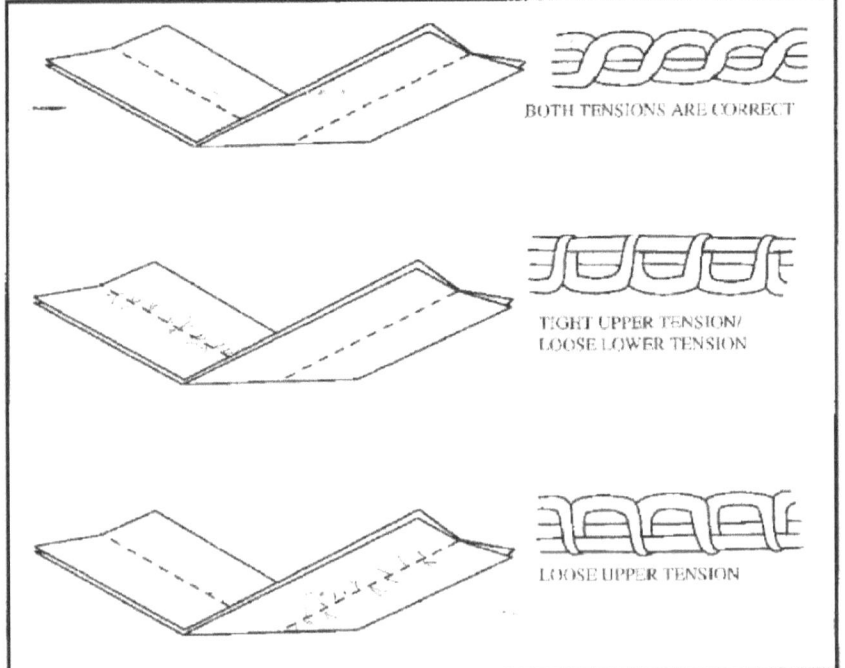

BOTH TENSIONS ARE CORRECT

TIGHT UPPER TENSION/
LOOSE LOWER TENSION

LOOSE UPPER TENSION

Figure 3-6. Thread tension

3-8. To test thread tension, stitch diagonally across a piece of scrap material. Look at the stitches closely. If the stitches do not look the same on both sides of the cloth, hold the stitching at each end and pull until a thread breaks. If the top thread breaks, there is too much tension on the top thread. If the bottom thread breaks, there is too much tension on the bottom thread. Follow the directions in the appropriate technical manual to adjust the thread tension on each sewing machine.

SECTION III – Tacking

3-9. Tacking (Figure 3-7) is used to secure the beginning and end of every seam. It keeps the cut ends of the thread from unraveling and the entire seam from pulling out. Tacking is sometimes called backstitching. Do not confuse it with the hand-sewn backstitch. There are two ways to tack seams with a sewing machine. The one used depends on whether or not the machine has the mechanism that allows it to sew in reverse.

Machine without a Reverse

3-10. Many older sewing machines do not have a reverse. To tack a seam using this type of machine—

- Place the cloth under the needle so that the bulk of the fabric is to the right of the needle and the seam allowance is to the left. Move the cloth until about 1 inch of the cloth lies in front of the needle. Adjust the cloth so that the needle will stitch the tacking on the same line that it will later stitch the seam.

- Lower the presser foot. To tack the beginning of the seam, sew a row of stitches about 1 inch long toward the cut edge of the cloth. Do not run off the cut edge of the cloth, but stop with the needle down in the fabric.

- Raise the presser foot. Pivot the cloth so that the seam can be sewn over the tacking stitches. The bulk of the fabric should now be to the left of the needle. The seam allowance should be to the right.

- Lower the presser foot. Stitch back over the tacking. Continue to sew to the end of the seam or the cut edge of the cloth. Do not run off the edge, but stop sewing with the needle down in the cloth.

- Raise the presser foot. Pivot the material on the needle.

- Lower the presser foot. Stitch back 1 inch over the seam stitches to tack the end of the seam.

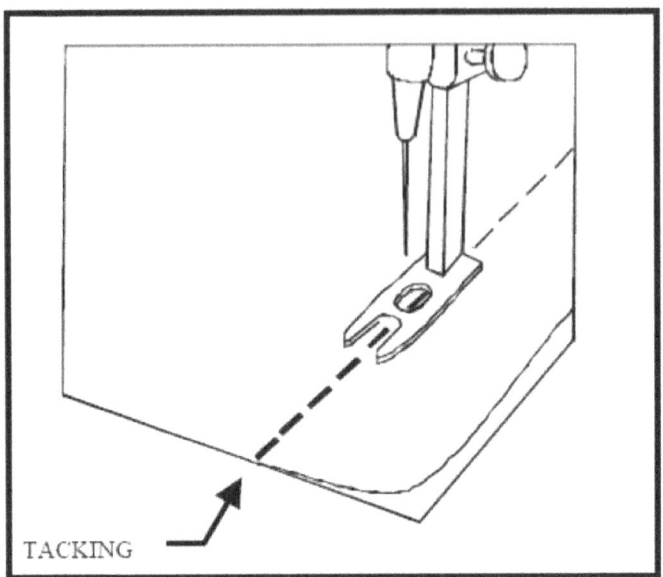

Figure 3-7. Tacking

Machine with a Reverse

3-11. The reverse mechanism is put into action by pushing a button or lever while the machine is working. Pushing the lever or button reverses the motion of the feed dogs. Material is fed back toward the operator instead of forward and away from the operator. Releasing the button or lever stops the reverse motion. To tack a seam using this type of machine—

- Place the cloth under the needle about 1 inch from the beginning of the seam line. Adjust the cloth so that the needle will stitch the tacking on the seam line. The bulk of the fabric should be to the left of the needle. The seam allowance will be to the right.
- Activate the reverse mechanism and sew back almost to the cut edge of the cloth. This tacks the seam at the beginning.
- Release the lever or button to stop the reverse mechanism and sew forward almost to the end of the seam line.
- Activate the reverse mechanism again, and sew back about 1 inch. This tacks the seam at the end.

SECTION IV – Characteristics of Good Seams

3-12. A seam is a row of stitches joining two or more pieces of material. Good seams have the following characteristics.

- Seams are as strong as the material they join in. Some seams are stronger than others because of the way they are constructed. Other factors affecting the strength of the seams are the type and length of the thread.

28

- Seams have just as much elasticity as the material they join. They do not break when the garment is put under stress. The elasticity of seams is determined by the thread and the type of stitch used to make the seams.
- Seams are durable and uniform in appearance. They do not have loose, crowded, tight, crooked, or skipped stitches. They do not have puckers or pleats.
- Seams are not wavy. Stitches are a uniform distance from the edge of the fabric. Raised seams do not have runoffs and felled seams do not have exposed raw edges.

SECTION V – Types of Seams

3-13. The military uses seven basic types of seams on clothing and textile items. At least two types of seams are used to make each piece of military clothing. The types of seams used depend on the garment, the location of the seams, and whether or not the seams are exposed.

Plain or Simple

3-14. The plain or simple seam (Figure 3-8) is the easiest seam to sew. It uses one row of stitches to join two pieces of cloth. This seam is used when a finished seam edge is not required, such as open side seams that must be mended. It is also used to mend straight and L-shaped tears when little or no material is missing. To make a simple seam—

- Place the material together face to face (all four edges square).
- Mark the edge of the material $\frac{1}{2}$ inch from the raw edge on the 8 inch length.
- Place the material on the machine so that the mark is in a vertical position.
- Start at the top of the marking on the edge of the material and stitch down to the bottom edge of the material. Allow a 1 inch tack stitch at both ends of the material not less than $\frac{7}{8}$-inch or more than 1 $\frac{1}{8}$ inches.
- Press the seams open with an iron.

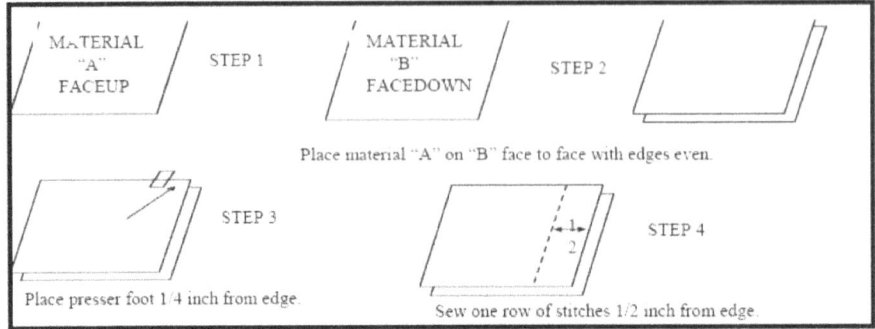

Figure 3-8. Simple Seam

Seam Type 1

3-15. Seam type 1 (Figure 3-9) is a hemming seam. It is used to put a machine-sewn hem in garments such as shirts and trousers. This seam is used when the garment does not need a deep or hidden hem. It is also used to put a simple finished seam edge on sheets and pillowcases and many other textile items. To make seam type 1—

- Place a piece of material 8 inches by 8 inches on the table face up.
- Mark the face side of the material 1 ½ inches from the edge (on the 8 inch edge), a straight line across the length of material.
- Make the second line ½ inch from the edge across the length of the material.
- Fold the material on the first mark made 1 ½ inches from the edge.
- Fold the material on the first mark made forming a hem. (The overall width of the hem when folded should be 1 inch at this time.)
- Place the material on the machine keeping the material folded.
- Starting on the end of the hem and on the ½ inch turn under, sew a row of stitches 1/16 inch from the folded edge, the length of the hem. Each end of the stitch line should be tacked.
- Press the material flat with an iron.

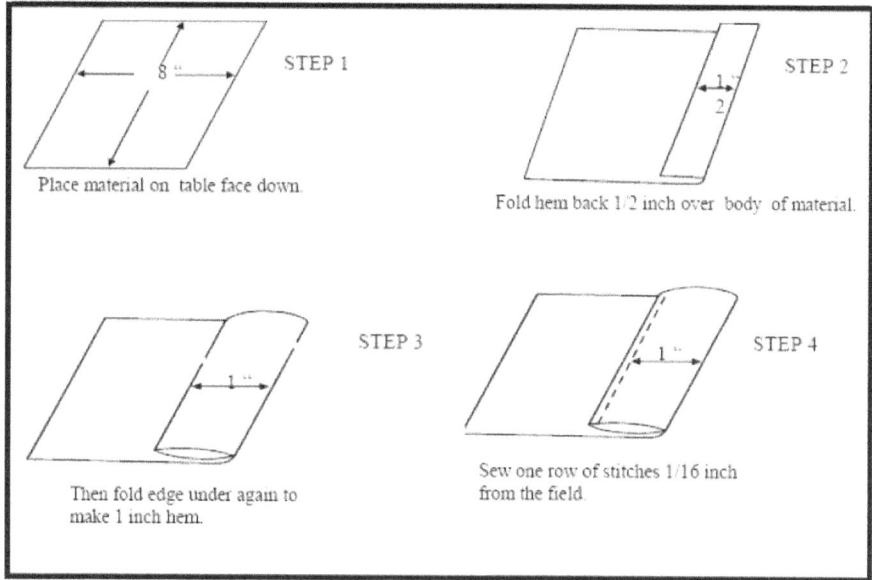

Figure 3-9. Seam type 1

Seam Type 2

3-16. Seam type 2 (Figure 3-10) is a lapped seam. It is used to sew a patch-type pocket on shirts, jackets, and coats. This seam is also used to sew plackets on shirt sleeves and to attach a zipper on the left side of a fly front. To make seam type 2—

- Cut an 8 by 8 inch piece of material into two pieces 4 inches by 8 inches.
- Place the two pieces of the material on a table face up.
- Mark both pieces of the material ½ inch from edge (on the 8 inches length) across length of material.
- Fold under edge of one piece of the material on the ½ inch mark and place it on the marking on the second piece of the material.
- Place the materials on the machine and stitch down the entire length of the material ¼ inch from the folded edge.
- Tack the stitch lines at both ends with a 1 inch tack (no less than ⅞ inch or no more than 1 ⅛ inches).
- Press the seam area with an iron.

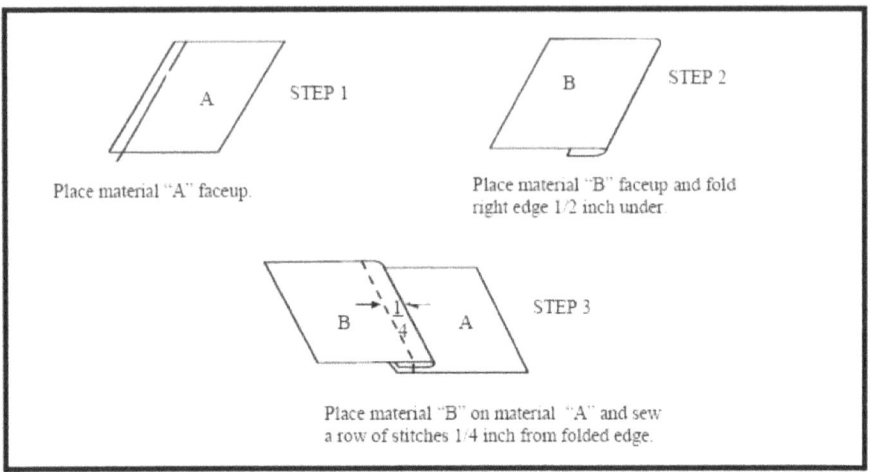

Figure 3-10. Seam type 2

Seam Type

3-17. Seam type 3 (Figure 3-11) is a welt seam. It is a strong seam used to sew pockets, sleeves, and main seams in heavy garments. This seam is also used to replace pocket flaps and to attach a zipper to the right side of a fly front. Seam type 3 is a combination of the simple seam and seam type 2. To make seam type 3—

- Cut an 8 by 8 inch piece of material into two pieces 4 inches by 8 inches.
- Place the two pieces of the material on the table face to face.
- Mark the top piece of material ½ inch from edge (on the 8 inch edge) across the length of material.
- Make certain both edges of the material (top and bottom pieces) are even at the marked edge.
- Sew the two pieces of material together with a simple seam, following the markings made ½ inch from the edge.
- Tack the stitch lines at both ends with a 1 inch tack (no less than ⅞ inch, or no more than 1/18 inches).
- Fold the top piece of the material to the right and sew a row of stitches ¼ inch to the right of the simple seam.
- Tack both ends of the seam with a 1 inch tack.
- Press the seam area flat with an iron.

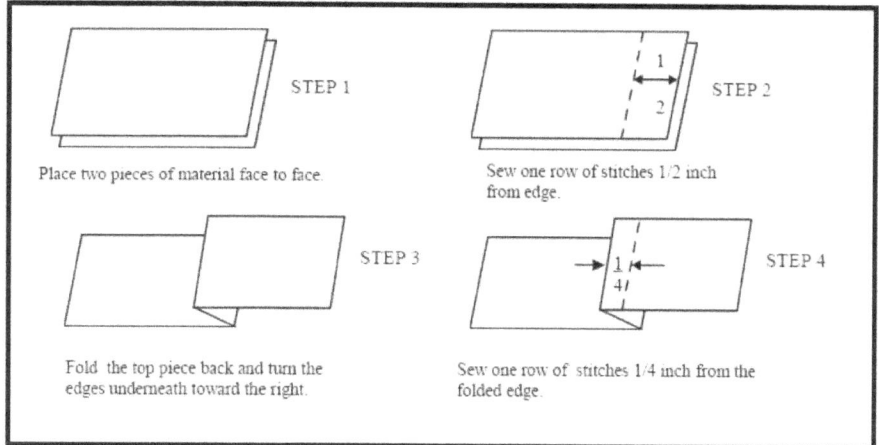

STEP 1

Place two pieces of material face to face.

STEP 2

Sew one row of stitches 1/2 inch from edge.

STEP 3

Fold the top piece back and turn the edges underneath toward the right.

STEP 4

Sew one row of stitches 1/4 inch from the folded edge.

Figure 3-11. Seam type 3

Seam Type 4

3-18. Seam type 4 (Figure 3-12) is a double-lapped seam. It is an extremely strong seam, because no raw edges are left exposed to unravel and two rows of stitches are used. This seam is used in garments that get a great deal of stress and are washed often. It is used to join the fronts and backs of shirts and field uniforms. When the seam is sewn correctly, it looks the same on the inside and the outside of the garment. To make seam type 4—

- Cut an 8- by 8-inch piece of material into two pieces 4 inches by 8 inches.
- Place the two pieces of the material face up and side by side.
- Mark the piece of the material on the left, ¼ inch from the right edge (8-inch length).
- Mark the piece of the material on the right, ½ inch from the left edge (8-inch length).
- Fold the material on the left ¼-inch mark and place it on the ½-inch mark of material on the right.
- Sew a row of stitches 1/16 inch from the folded edge of the top material. Make certain to tack both ends of the seam.
- Turn the joined materials over with the back side of the material up.
- Mark ¼ inch from the raw edge of the joined seam.
- Fold under ¼ inch at mark and stitch 1/16 inch from the folded edge across the length of the material.
- Tack at both ends of the seam with a 1-inch tack (no less than ⅞ inches, or no more than 1 ⅛ inches).
- Make sure that the stitch lines are evenly spaced and straight. Make sure each seam line has a tack at each end and that no raw edges are showing.

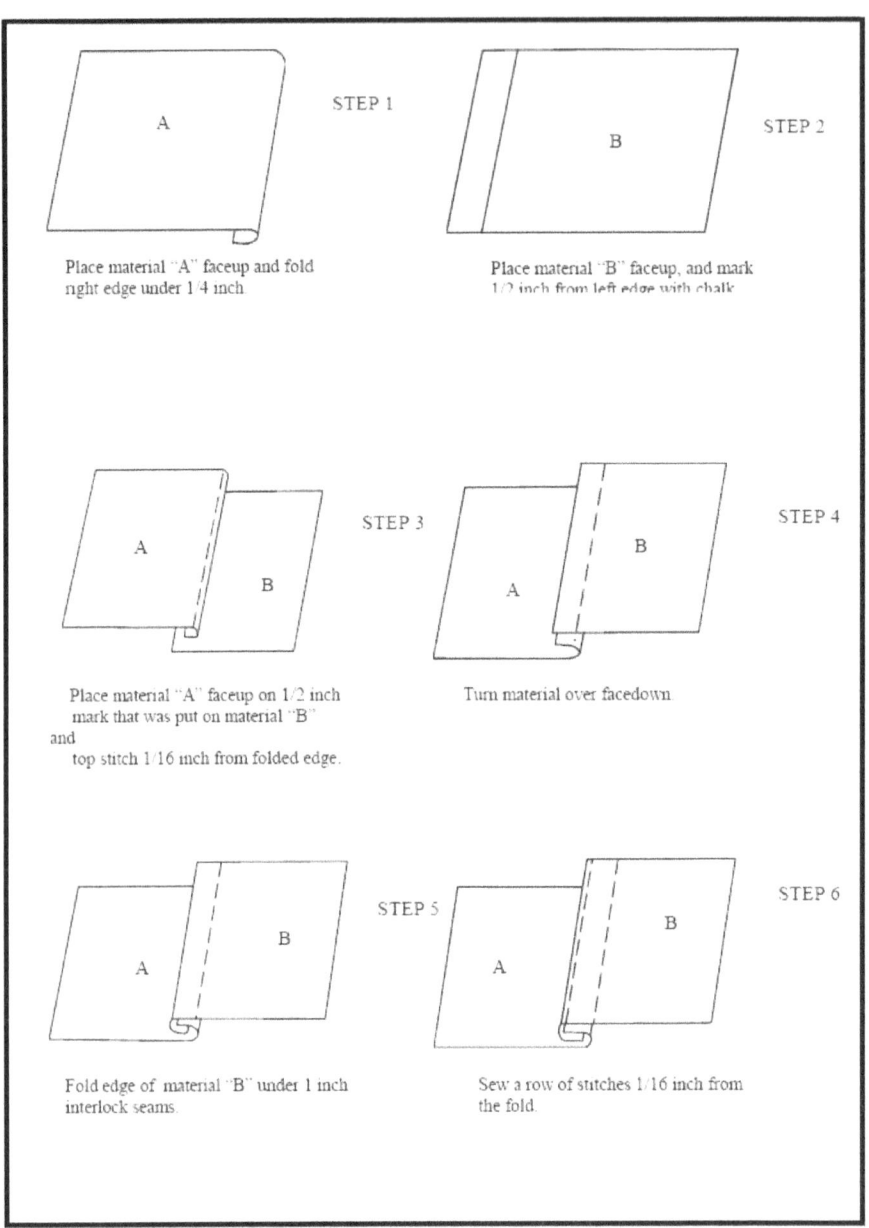

Figure 3-12. Seam type 4

Seam Type 5

3-19. Seam type 5 (Figure 3-13) is an overlapped and topstitched seam. It is used to attach collars and cuffs to shirts. To make seam type 5—

- Cut an 8 by 8 inch piece of material into two pieces 4 inches by 8 inches.
- Place both pieces of the material on the table face up and squarely over each other.
- Mark a line on the top piece of the material on the right side of material ½ inch from edge (8 inch length).

3-20. Sew both pieces of material together with a simple seam, following the markings made ½ inch from the edge. Tack the stitch lines at both ends with a 1 inch tack (no less than ⅞ inch or no more than 1 ⅛ inches).

- Fold the bottom piece of material to the right, ½-inch seams up and also folded to the right.
- Mark the edge of right material ½ inch from the edge (face side).
- Fold the edge of the material on the ½ inch markings. Fold material over so that the folded ½ inch edge overlaps the simple seam ⅛ inch.
- Sew a row of stitches 1/16 inch from the folded edge. Make certain to tack both ends of the seam (1 inch tack). No less than ⅞ inch or no more than 1 ⅛ inches.
- Press the seam area flat with an iron.

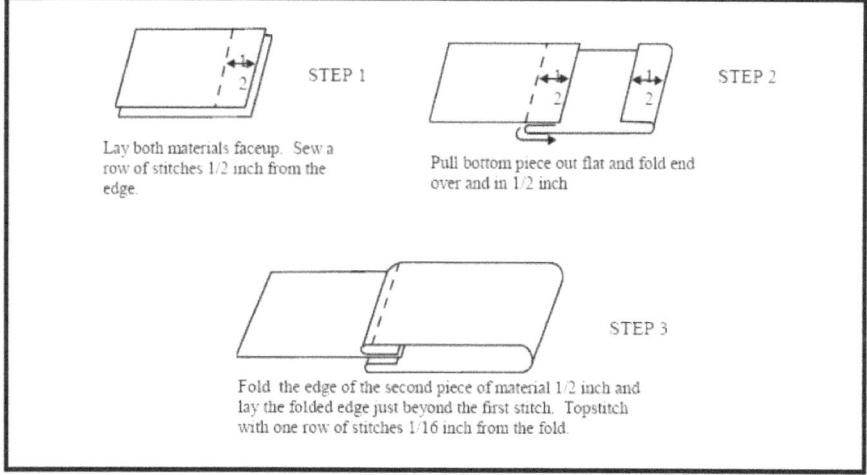

Lay both materials faceup. Sew a row of stitches 1/2 inch from the edge.

STEP 1

Pull bottom piece out flat and fold end over and in 1/2 inch

STEP 2

Fold the edge of the second piece of material 1/2 inch and lay the folded edge just beyond the first stitch. Topstitch with one row of stitches 1/16 inch from the fold.

STEP 3

Figure 3-13. Seam type 5

Seam Type 6

3-21. Seam type 6 (Figure 3-14) is a simple seam topstitched to enclose the raw edges. It is used to finish the edge on cuffs, collars, and pocket flaps. This seam is also used to sew welts on side pockets. To make seam type 6—

- Cut an 8- by 8-inches piece of material into two pieces 4 inches by 8 inches.
- Place the two pieces squarely over each other, and face to face.

- Mark the top piece of material ½ inch from the right edge (8 inch length).
- Make certain the marked edges are even.
- Join the two pieces of the material together by sewing with a simple seam. Tack the stitch lines at both ends with a 1 inch tack (no less than ⅞ inch, or no more than 1 ⅛ inches).
- Fold the bottom piece of the material to the right and press the seams open with an iron.
- Fold the right material over the left piece of material. (At this point, the simple seam is at the operator's right and the top material is face up).
- Mark the top material ¼ inch from the right edge (this is where the two materials are joined with a simple seam) across the length of material.
- Sew a row of stitches following the mark ¼ inch from the right edge of both pieces of the material. Make sure the stitching is straight and evenly spaced ¼ inch from the edge).
- Make sure each seam line has a 1-inch tack at both ends (no less than ⅞ inch, no more than 1 ⅛ inches).
- Press the seam area flat with an iron.

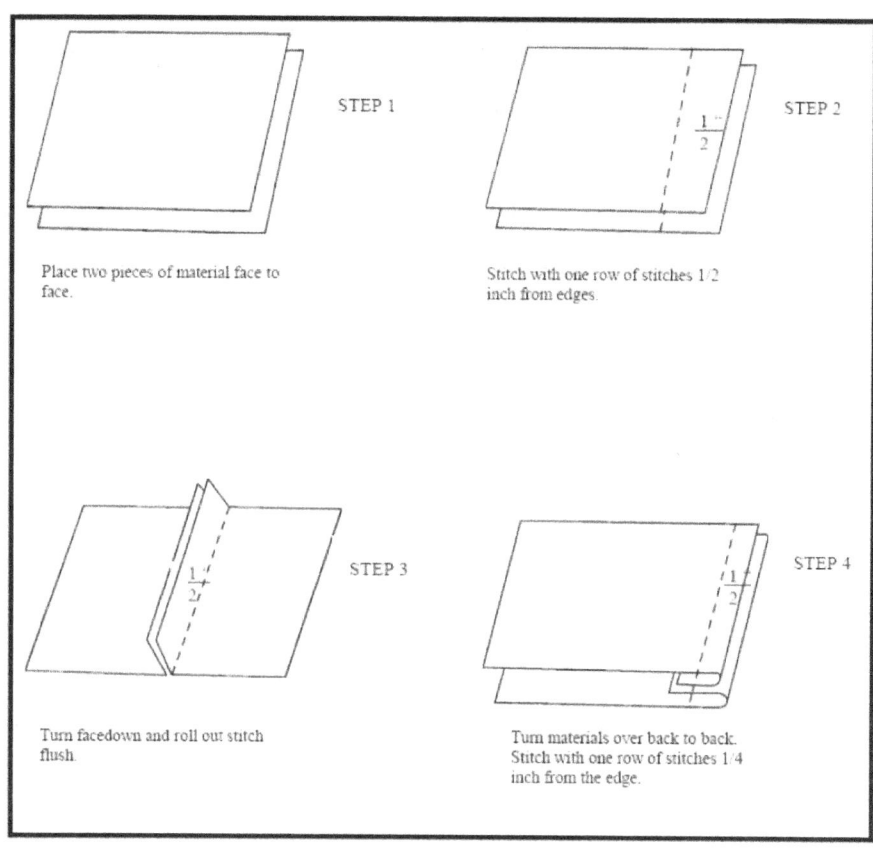

Figure 3-14. Seam type 6

CHAPTER 4 – REPAIRING CLOTHING & TEXTILE ITEMS

SECTION I – Preparing Supplies & Equipment

4-1. The fabric repair specialist repairs the defects noted during the initial inspection of a garment or textile item. When the fabric repair specialist receives a defective item, he first searches for the chalk marks made by the initial inspector to identify needed repairs. The fabric repair specialist then obtains the necessary tools and supplies to make those repairs. He gets the correct size, type, and color zippers, buttons, thread, and patch material. The fabric repair specialist may have to adjust the sewing machine to make specific repairs. These repairs include darning, patching, re-stitching hems and open seams, replacing worn cuffs, collars, and pockets; mending buttonholes; and replacing zippers, buttons, elastic, buckles, eyelets, and snaps.

SECTION II – Darning

4-2. Darning is used to reinforce small areas that have worn thin from use and repeated washing. Darns are used to repair small holes that are less than 1 inch wide. They are also used to repair slits and straight tears where no fabric is missing. Darns are made using thread that matches or is similar to the color and weight of that used to weave the cloth. Perfectly matched darns can be made by hand using thread which has been unraveled from a seam allowance or the hem of a garment that is not repairable. Darns are made by hand and by darning machines or sewing machines. See the appropriate technical manual for instructions on how to operate each machine. There are four kinds of darns. The kind used on a certain item depends on the extent of the repair to be made.

Circular Darn

4-3. A circular darn (Figure 4-1) is used to repair very small holes and worn spots. To make a circular darn—

- Turn the cloth so it is face up.
- Start sewing just outside the damaged area. Stitch first around the area. Then stitch toward the center in a spiral fashion. Make the stitches close together but do not overlap them.
- Stitch around and around, making the spiral smaller and smaller until the stitches reach the center.

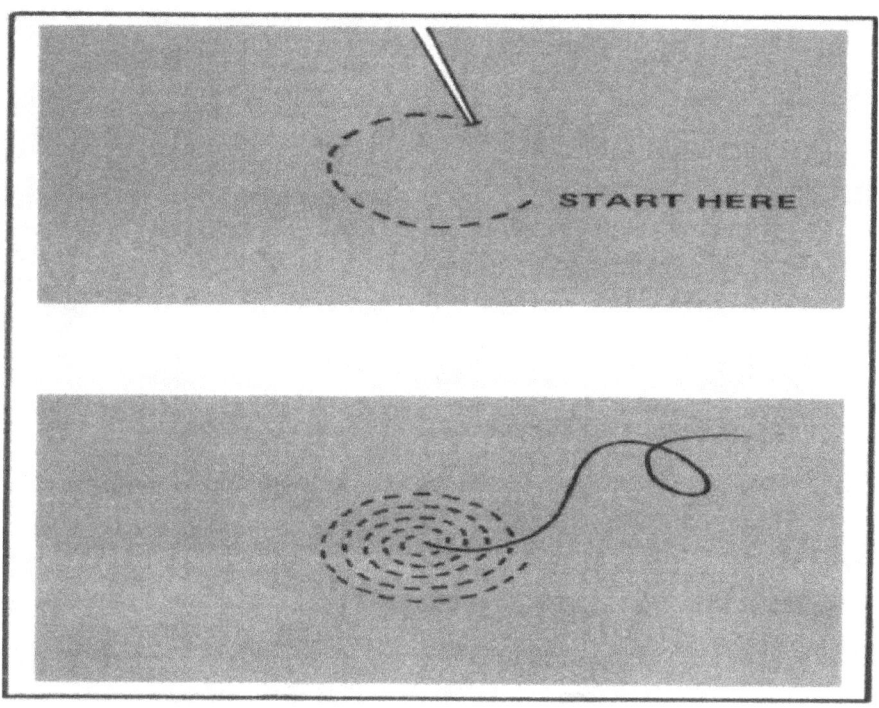

Figure 4-1. Circular darn

One-Way Darn

4-4. The one-way darn (Figure 4-2) is used to repair small worn areas of cloth where either the vertical or horizontal threads have worn away and left the other threads loose. To make a one-way darn—

- Turn the cloth face up.
- Start and end the stitching in the undamaged area about ¼ inch from the worn spot.
- Stitch back and forth either horizontally or vertically across the worn spot to replace the missing threads. Stitch all rows parallel and as close together as possible without overlapping them.

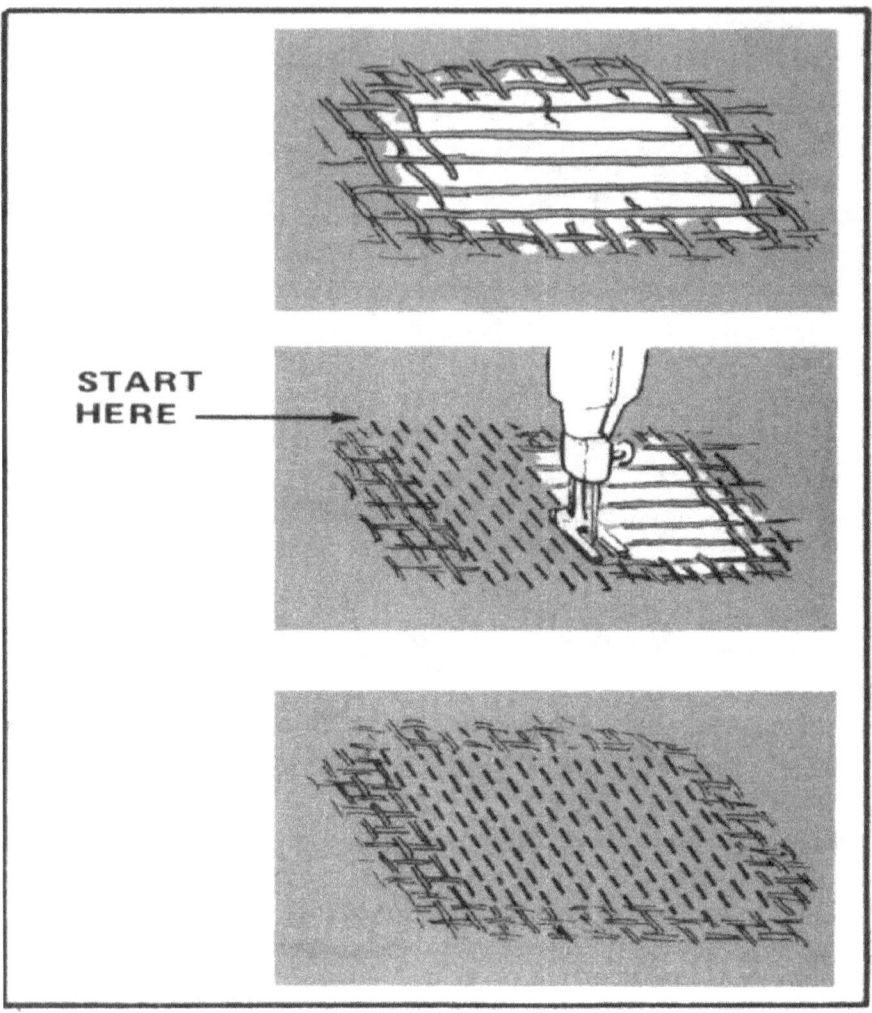

START
HERE

Figure 4-2. One-way darn

Zigzag Darn

4-5. The zigzag darn (Figure 4-3) is used to repair holes that are less than ½ inch across. It is also used to repair slits and straight tears where no fabric is missing. To make a zigzag darn—

- Turn the cloth face up. To fix a hole, first flatten out the edges around the hole. To fix a tear, first draw a rectangular box around the tear ¼ inch away from the tear on all sides with tailor's clay chalk.

- Start and end the stitching in the undamaged area around the hole or on either end of the tear.

- Stitch back and forth across the damaged area in a zigzag fashion, covering the hole or filling in the rectangle. Stitch the rows as close together as possible without overlapping them. Do not stitch outside the lines of the rectangle.

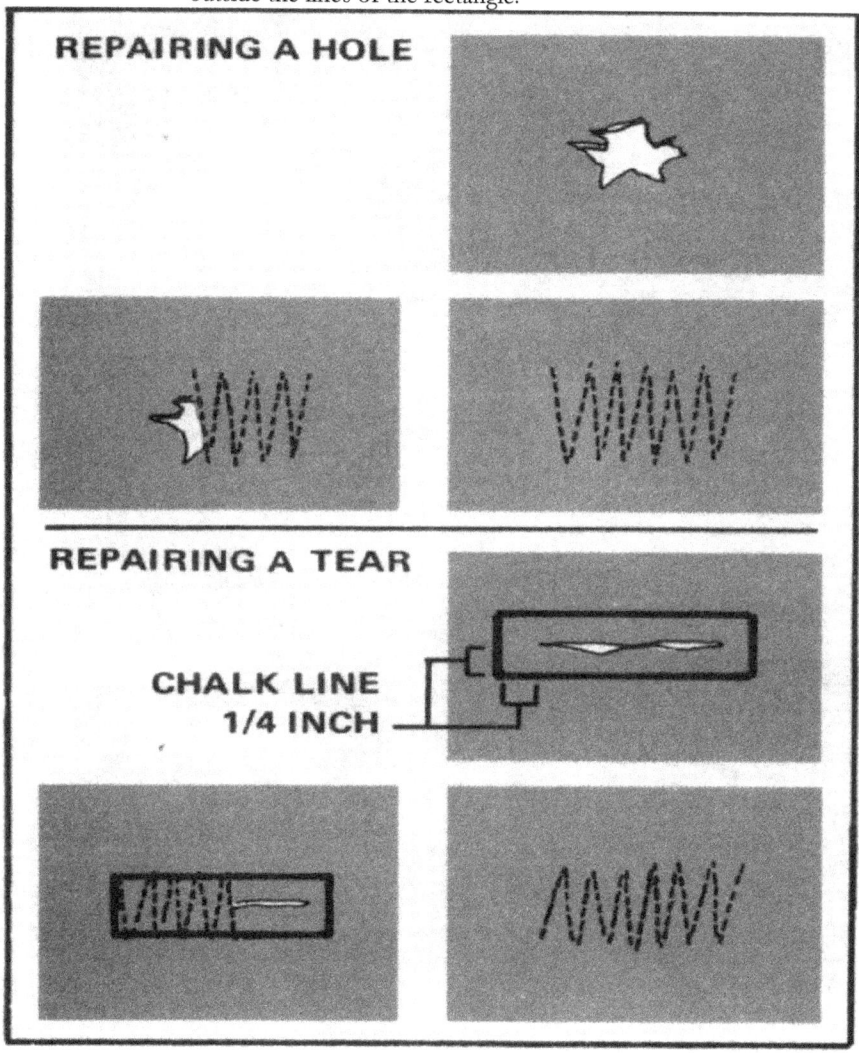

Figure 4-3. Zigzag darn

Reinforced Darn

4-6. The reinforced darn (Figure 4-4) is used to repair holes from ½ inch to 1 inch across. To make a reinforced darn—

- Turn the garment or textile item so that the damaged area is face up.

- Measure ¼ inch on each side of the hole and draw a rectangle around the damage with tailor's clay chalk.
- Place a scrap piece of matching fabric face up under the hole.
- Stitch back and forth across the hole and through the reinforcing fabric in a zigzag fashion. Completely fill in the rectangle with close rows of stitches.
- Turn the garment or textile item over so that it is face down. If necessary, trim any excess matching fabric to within ¼ inch of the darn.

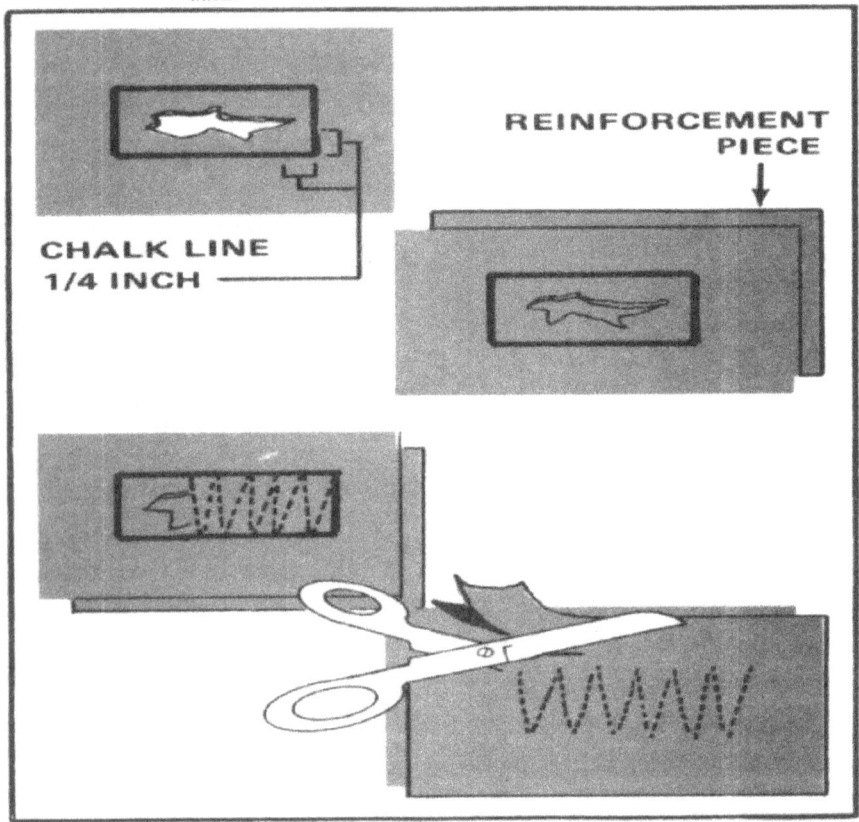

Figure 4-4. Reinforced darn

SECTION III – Patching

4-7. Patching is used to repair holes larger than 1 inch across. It is also used to repair L-shaped tears and to mend large worn areas of cloth. Patches are cut from scrap fabric which exactly matches the cloth to be mended. They are usually rectangular in shape. The straight grain of the patch is aligned with the straight grain of the cloth to be repaired. The goal is to make the patch blend in with the cloth. There are several different kinds of patches. All are sewn on except the iron-on patch.

Simple Clothing Patch

4-8. A simple clothing patch is sewn over or under a damaged area. The damaged area is then cut away, and the raw edges are turned under and stitched down. There are two kinds of simple clothing patches.

Top Patch

4-9. A top patch (Figure 4-5) is sewn to the outside of a garment or to the top of a textile item. This patch is a piece of material that matches the item being repaired and is cut at least 2 ½ inches larger on all sides than the hole or damaged area to be covered. To apply this patch--

- Place the damaged area of the item on the table face up.
- Center the patch over the damaged area, face up, so that the grain of the patch matches the grain of the item.
- Turn the edges of the patch under ½ inch. Stitch 1/16 inch from, and all around, the edge of the patch. Tack not less than ⅞ inch or not more than 1 ⅛ inches.
- Turn the item over and cut out the hole or damaged area so that it is square or rectangular.
- Notch the corners of the damaged material to ½ inch.
- Fold the raw edges of the notched material ½ inch and press the edges.
- Stitch 1/16 inch from, and all around, the folded edges.
- Tack not less than ⅞ inch and not more than 1 ⅛ inches.

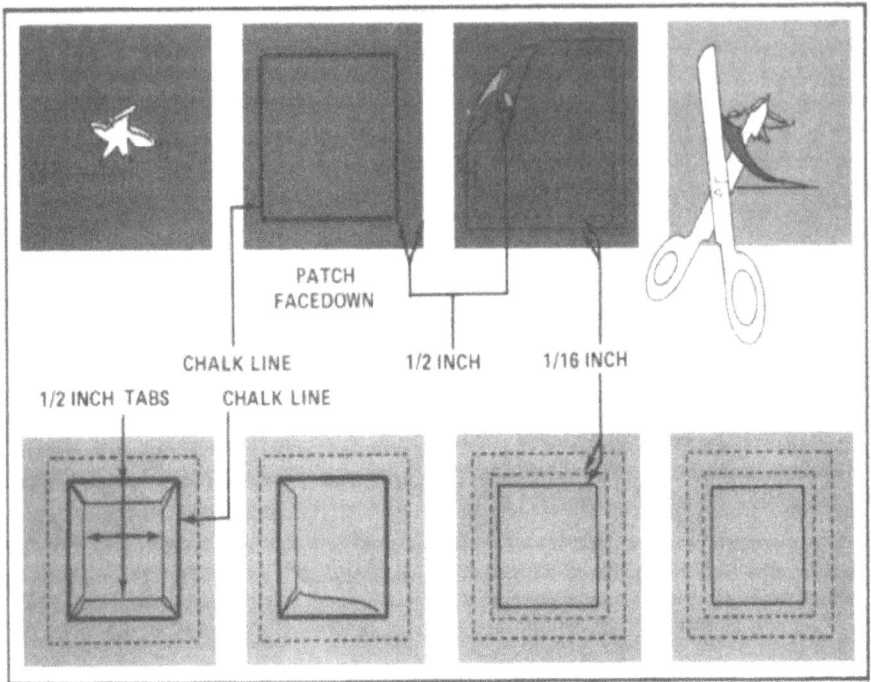

Figure 4-5. Top patch

PATCH
FACEDOWN

CHALK LINE   1/2 INCH   1/16 INCH

1/2 INCH TABS   CHALK LINE

Inverted Patch

4-10. This patch is applied in the same manner as the top patch except that this patch is sewn to the underside of the item rather than the outside.

Set-in Patch

4-11. The set-in patch (Figure 4-6) is not like a top patch or inverted patch, which is sewn on or under a damaged area. A set-in patch takes the place of a damaged area. The damaged area is cut out, and then a set-in patch is tailor-made to fit the hole. A set-in patch is used when a less noticeable patch is needed. To make a set-in patch—

- Place two pieces of material on the table face up.
- Mark materials A and B. Material A represents the damaged area. Material B represents the patch.
- On material A, cut out a 4 inch square from the center of the damaged area. This is done by marking 2 inches from all edges of the damage and mark off a square. Allow ½ inch for seaming purpose.
- Notch all four corners of the square at a 45-degree angle.
- Place and center material A over material B (materials are face up).
- Starting on the right side of the materials, fold under the notched seams of material A in such a manner that the seam is to the

44

operator's right and the body of the material to the operator's left. At this point, the right side of material A, the underside, is shown up.

- Start at the upper portion of the notched seam and sew down to the bottom notch. The beginning and end of the stitch line should be one stitch length in from the corner of the notch. (This will prevent any raw edge from showing when completed.)

- Continue to sew the remaining three edges of material A to material B in the same manner as shown in the step above.

- Cut and trim excess material from material B to coincide with the edges of seams on material A.

- Turn materials flat with the underside up, and open seams. For best results, use an iron to press open.

- Turn materials over face up, starting on the right side of the material A and 1/16 inch from the seam line; stitch a row of stitches around the square.

- When reaching the starting point of the stitch line, cross over the seam line the length of two stitches to material B, continue the second stitch line around the square 1/16 inch from seam. Make certain to tack with a 1 inch tack at the end of the stitch line.

- Press the completed set-in patch with an iron.

Note: During the construction of the set-in patch, it is important that the stitch rows be applied straight, a slight curving of the stitch lines will cause the materials to pull or pucker when completed.

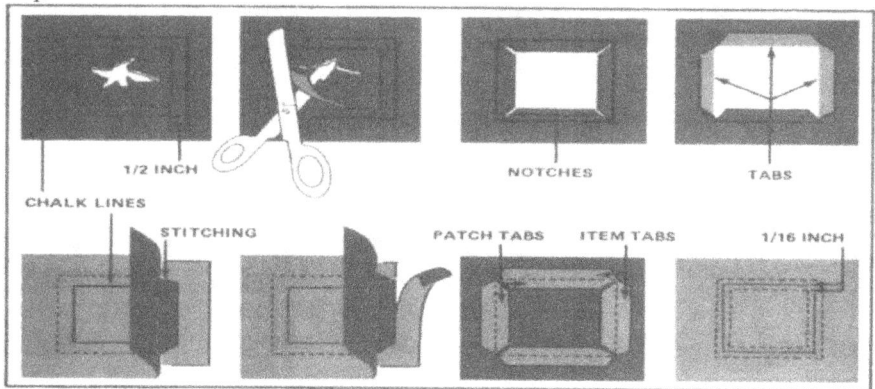

Figure 4-6. Set-in patch

T-Patch

4-12. The T-patch (Figure 4-7) is used to repair L-shaped tears. Unlike the other patches, the T-patch does not require an additional piece of cloth. To make a T-patch—

- Enlarge by cutting the L-shaped tear so that it forms an inverted T.

- Place the item on the table, face up, so that the T is inverted. Fold the right edge of the material to the left along the vertical tear.
- Sew a row of stitches, beginning 1 inch above the end of the vertical tear at the edge of the fold, and continue to the horizontal tear ending stitches ¼ inch from the edge of the vertical tear. Tack seam at the beginning and the end.
- Rotate the item to the left ¼ turn so that the horizontal tear is now vertical. Fold the right edge of material to the left along the horizontal tear.
- Sew a row of stitches, beginning 1 inch above the end of the horizontal tear at the edge of the fold, and continue to the juncture of the vertical tear, so that the seam at this point is ¼ inch from the edge of the horizontal tear. Continue sewing until the row of stitches ends 1 inch below the bottom end of tear at the edge of the fold. Tack the seam at beginning and end.
- Turn the item over so that the face side is down. Spread the edges of the tears away from seams, and press flat using an iron.
- Turn the item over so that the face side is up. Sew a row of stitches 1/16 inch from and around seams. Tack the row of stitches at the beginning and the end.

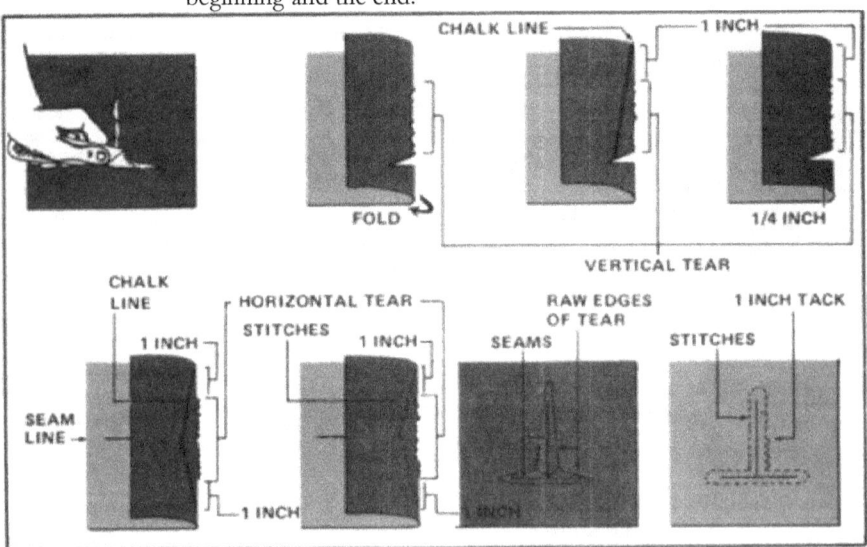

Figure 4-7. T-patch

Iron-On Patch

4-13. The iron-on patch (Figure 4-8) may be used to repair sleeping bags. It can be used instead of a pinch patch to repair small holes and tears. To apply an iron-on patch—

- Replace any missing insulation.
- Trim unraveled ends and measure the damaged area.

46

- Cut a patch from iron-on patching material. Make the patch large enough to extend ½ inch beyond the damaged area on all four sides. Round off the corners of the patch.

- Unzip the sleeping bag. Place the damaged area on a flat, hard surface that heat will not affect.

- Shake or move the underlying insulation away from the damaged area.

- Smooth out and warm the damaged area by pressing with a dry iron set on cotton. Do not scorch the fabric.

- Quickly cover the damaged area with the iron-on patch.

- Hold the iron on the patch. Apply constant pressure for 8 seconds, moving the iron back and forth slightly. If the patch is larger than the iron, press the patch section by section, starting in the center.

- Allow the patch to cool for at least 5 seconds before moving the sleeping bag.

- After the patch has cooled for 5 minutes, test the patch by trying to lift one of the corners with a fingernail. If a ¼ to ½ inch section of the corner comes loose, try to peel off the patch. A well-bonded patch will be hard to remove. A poorly bonded patch will peel off easily. Re-press a poorly bonded patch using a hotter iron, but do not scorch the patch or the fabric. Increase the pressing and cooling times. Test and re-press the patch until it is hard to remove. Re-press the tested corner.

Note. If a patch fails to stick after several pressings, use a new patch.

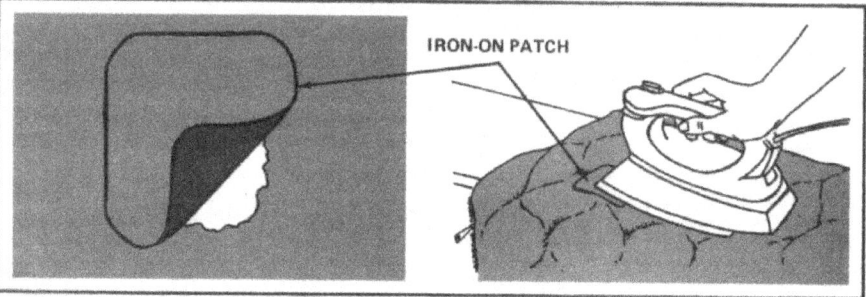

Figure 4-8. Iron-on patch

Iron-On Patches of Garments

4-14. Rips and tears other than stress points (e.g., crotch seams, pocket seams, pocket flap seams, etc.) may be repaired by iron-on patches. Any rip or tears closer than ¾ (1.91 cm) to any seam will be repaired by sewing. Iron-on patches are suitable for use on the utility shirt and trousers when garment appearance is not first priority. To apply an iron-on patch--

- Cut the patch to the size and shape that it will extend approximately ¾ inch (1.91 cm) in all directions beyond the tear or other damage. Patches will have rounded corners.

47

- When patching by hand iron, place patch center and to the inside of the garment.
- Trim the heavily raveled ends with scissors.
- Smooth out the area to be patched to prevent wrinkles, folds, seams, or other protrusions under the iron when it is applied.
- Pre-warm the area to be patched by pressing with a dry iron set at cotton or as high as possible without scorching the fabric; apply the iron for 5 seconds or more.
- Immediately position the patch. Hold the iron on the patch for about 12 seconds.
- Use no more than a slight rotation motion on the iron and apply constant pressure.
- Remove the iron and allow the patched area to cool in place about 5 seconds or long enough so that the patch will not drift off when the garment is removed from the iron board. If the adhesive strikes through the patch cloth, too much heat has been applied. Reduce time of pressing or temperature of the iron. A small amount of strike through is not objectionable provided the patch meets the check test described in *4-3d(10)*.

A bonded patch, which has a lifted edge, will be re-ironed. A bonded patch that has been subjected to the check test will be replaced.

Note: When patching by special automatic press, the platen temperature, dwell time, dwell pressure and other details shall be in accordance with the press manufacturer's instructions.

SECTION IV – Replacing Buttons

4-15. Buttons have two uses. Their functional purpose is to close openings on clothing and textile items. Their decorative purpose is to provide a finishing touch to enhance the appearance of military uniforms. There are two kinds of buttons. Flat or sew-through buttons have two or four holes (Figure 4-9). They are used as fasteners on lightweight garments. Shank buttons (Figure 4-9) have shanks or stems which lift the buttons off the surface of the cloth to which they are attached. Shank buttons are used on heavyweight garments because the shank permits a thicker layer of cloth to fit between the button and the underlying cloth. If more space is needed between the button and the garment, a thread shank can be used with either button. Buttons are attached to garments with a button-sewing machine or by hand sewing. Directions for operating a button-sewing machine are included in the technical manual for the machine. Directions for attaching buttons by hand are given below.

General Directions

4-16. When making button repairs—
- Re-stitch all loose buttons.
- Replace broken buttons with identical, undamaged ones.
- Replace missing buttons with buttons that are the same type, color, and size as the missing ones.

- Sew a replacement button in the same spot the previous button was sewn. If this spot is not obvious, overlap the edges of the garment and stick a straight pin through the buttonhole of the missing button and into the underlying cloth. For horizontal buttonholes, stick the pin in ⅛ inch from the end closest to the edge of the garment. For a vertical buttonhole, stick the pin ⅛-inch down from the top.
- If the underlying cloth has been torn, repair the cloth with a reinforced darn before attaching a button in the same spot.
- Use the same kind of thread that was used to attach the other buttons to the garment or textile items. In most cases, the thread will be buttonhole twist thread. Thread the needle with a 1 yard length of thread. Draw the thread through the eye of the needle until the two ends are even, and knot the ends together.
- Insert the needle up through the underside of the cloth to hide the knot. Make several stitches on top of each other to anchor the thread before attaching the button.

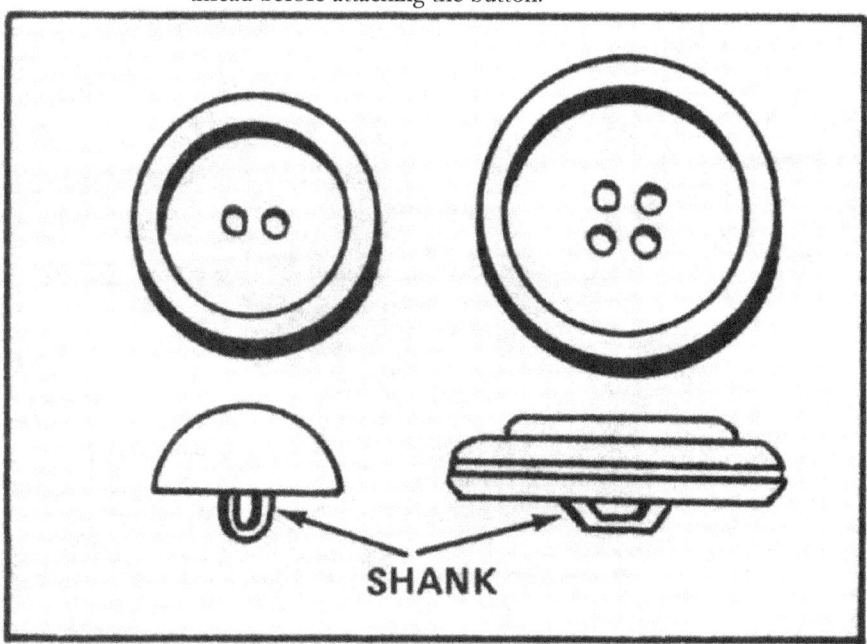

Figure 4-9. Sew-through and shank buttons

Direction for Attaching Sew-Through Buttons

4-17. Sew-through buttons are attached by hand using one of two methods. One method sews the button directly on the cloth. The other method uses a thread shank between the button and cloth.

Without a Thread Shank

4-18. To sew a sew-through button flat to a garment or textile item—

- Anchor the thread, and then stick the needle up through one of the holes in the button. Slide the button down the length of the thread.
- For a two-hole button, stick the needle down through the other hole and through the underlying cloth. Pull the needle and thread through to the other side.
- Stick the needle up through the first hole again and go down through the second hole. Repeat this step four times.
- Knot the thread close to the cloth on the reverse side and cut off the remaining thread close to the knot.
- For a four-hole button, stitch through one pair of holes and then through the other pair so that the stitches are parallel.

With a Thread Shank

4-19. To sew on a sew-through button with a thread shank, use one of the following methods.

- Fold the cloth over the index finger. Hold the button against the cloth with the thumb. Sew on the buttons following the steps above. On the last stitch, go down through the button, but do not penetrate the cloth. Flatten out the cloth and grasp the button. Wind the thread around the stitches several times to make a shank. Take one stitch through the bottom of the shank to secure the thread. Stick the needle through the cloth to the reverse side. Knot the thread close to the cloth, and cut off the remaining thread close to the knot.
- Stick the needle up through one of the holes and slide the button down the length of the thread. Lay one or two straight pins across the top of the button and hold them in place with the thumb. Sew on the button, stitching across the straight pins. On the last stitch, go down through the button, but do not penetrate the cloth. Remove the pins and lift the button away from the cloth. Wind the thread around the stitches to make a shank. Take one stitch through the button of the shank to secure the thread. Stick the needle through the cloth to the reverse side. Knot the thread close to the cloth and cut the remaining thread close to the knot.

Directions for Attaching Shank Buttons

4-20. Shank buttons are attached by hand using one of two methods. One method sews the shank flat to the cloth. The other method adds an additional shank made from thread.

Without a Thread Shank

4-21. To attach a shank button without an additional thread shank--

- Position the button so that the shank aligns with the buttonhole and so the stitches will be parallel to the edge of the opening in the garment.
- Anchor the thread and then stick the needle through the hole in the shank.
- Stick the needle down through the cloth and pull the thread through to the inside.
- Stick the needle up through the cloth, through the hole in the shank, and down through the cloth again. Repeat this step six times.
- Knot the thread close to the cloth and cut the remaining thread close to the knot.

With a Thread Shank

4-22. To attach a shank button with a thread shank--

- Follow the steps above to attach button. During stitching, hold the tip of the forefinger between the button and the cloth to keep the two apart.
- On the last stitch, pass the thread through the hole in the shank, but do not penetrate the cloth.
    o Grasp the button and wrap the thread around the stitches to form a shank. Take one stitch through the bottom of the shank.
    o Stick the needle and thread through the cloth to the inside. Knot the thread close to the cloth, and cut the remaining thread close to the knot.

SECTION V – Remaking Buttonholes

4-23. Buttonholes are small horizontal or vertical openings through which buttons are passed. The length of the buttonholes depends on the size of their buttons. Properly sized buttonholes are long enough for their buttons to slip through easily and short enough to prevent the buttons from coming undone accidentally. Generally, buttonholes are ¼ inch longer than the width of the buttons. The buttonholes used on military garments are keyhole buttonholes. They have eyes to keep the buttonholes from becoming distorted by button shanks. Even though the edges of all buttonholes are reinforced to prevent damage, repeated use and washing wear them out. The threads unravel, the edges fray, and the surrounding cloth tears. Damaged buttonholes look ragged and are usually too large to hold buttons properly in place. Buttonholes can be repaired by using a sewing machine or by hand sewing. Instructions for making machine-worked buttonholes can be found in appropriate technical manuals. To remake a buttonhole by hand—

- Remove the old stitches around the buttonhole.
- Close the buttonhole with a reinforced darn.

- Use a buttonhole cutter to cut a slit ¼ inch longer than the width of the button. Cut the slit in the same place as the previous buttonhole.
- Cut an eye in one end of the buttonhole. If the buttonhole is vertical, cut the eye in the top of the slit. If the buttonhole is horizontal, cut the eye in the end closer to the finished edge of the garment.
- Use a buttonhole stitch to finish the cut edges of the buttonhole.
- Start stitching at the end that does not have the eye. Stitch along one edge, fan the stitches out around the eye, and stitch back along the other edge.
- Secure the buttonhole stitches by taking three or four long stitches straight across the width of the two rows of the buttonhole stitches.
- Stick the needle and thread through the cloth to the inside. Cut the remaining thread close to the knot.

SECTION VI – Replacing Zippers

4-24. A zipper is called a slide fastener in supply catalogs. The military uses two kinds of zippers, separating and non-separating. A separating zipper (Figure 4-10) opens completely. The left side splits away from the right side when the end of the left side is lifted out of the slide. The non-separating zipper (Figure 4-11) does not come apart completely. The left side is permanently attached to the right side at the bottom of the zipper. Repeated use and washing damage zippers.

4-25. The cloth tears, the metal teeth rust or come loose. The slide jams and will not move up or down. The slide is lost. The fabric repair specialist replaces these broken zippers with new or salvaged ones. Replacement zippers should be the same type, size, and color as the broken zippers. Directions are given here for replacing the non-separating zipper in a trouser and the separating zipper in a jacket. Replacing others may differ slightly from these two examples. The key point to remember is that a replacement zipper is sewn in place in the same way the previous zipper was sewn in place. A fabric repair specialist examines a garment or textile item and notes how the zipper was sewn in before attempting to replace it.

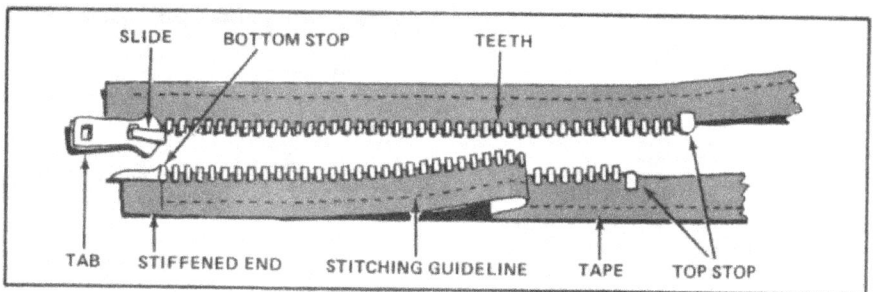

Figure 4-10. Separating zipper

Replacing a Non-Separating Zipper in Trousers

4-26. To remove zipper from trousers (Figure 4-12)—

- Start at the left side of the fly and rip stitches. (Start at top, work down as far as the tacking stitch bottom of the fly.)
- Where the zipper is tucked under at the waistband, rip just enough stitches to remove the end of the zipper.
- In cutting the stitches, take necessary precautions not to damage the trouser material.
- Cut stitches and remove the zipper from the fly on the right side of trouser.
- Cut and remove the stitches from the fly facing.
- Cut the stitches from bar tack at the bottom of the fly and remove the zipper.
- Do not cut below or beyond the tacking stitches.

4-27. To prepare trouser and zipper for replacement—

- Remove all old loose stitches from the trouser fly.
- Select a zipper of the proper size and length. Make sure the color and shade of the zipper match.

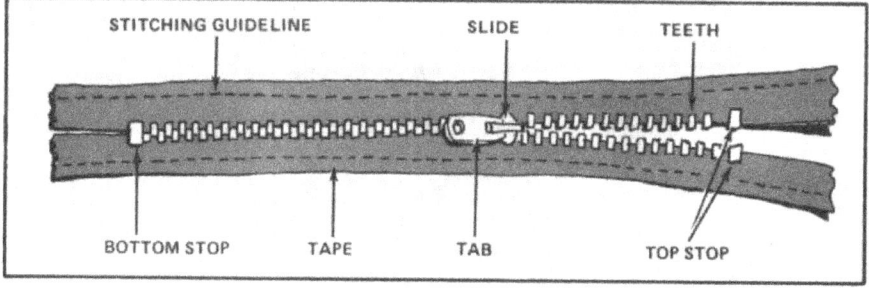

Figure 4-11. Non-separating Zipper

4-28. To replace the zipper to the trouser—

- Pin the zipper to the fly facing and sew the zipper to the facing.
- Follow the same procedure on the left side of the fly. Make certain the zipper is aligned.

- Sew the facing to trousers; make certain to follow the old stitch line.
- Stitch the waist band to the trouser fly, securing the zipper.
- Replace the tacking stitch at the bottom of the fly.

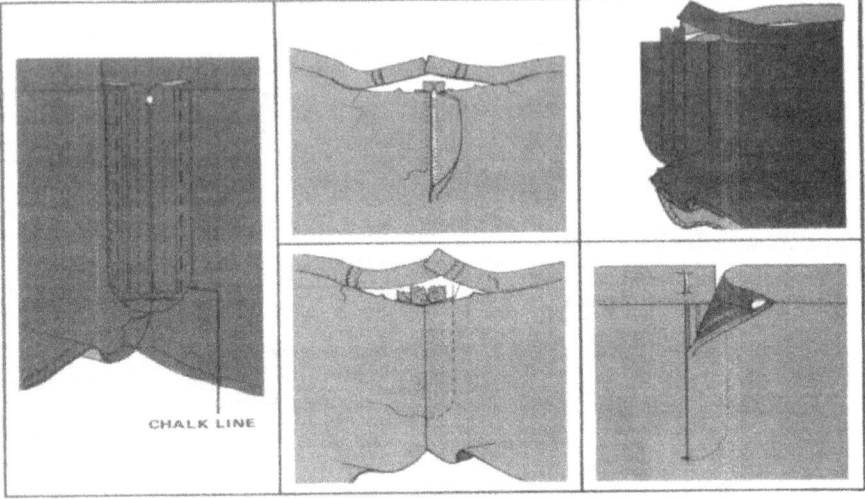

Figure 4-12. Replacing zipper on trousers

Replacing a Separating Zipper in Jacket

4-29. To replace a separating zipper in a jacket—
- Place the jacket face up on the table and close the zipper. If the zipper will not close, line up the edges exactly and pin the zipper in place.
- Obtain a matching replacement zipper.
- Turn the jacket inside out.
- Place the replacement zipper face down directly on the old zipper. Match the position exactly.
- Draw several horizontal lines with tailor's clay chalk on each side of the new zipper. Draw the lines across the zipper tape and the cloth in the garment. Use these index marks as guides to position the new zipper.
- Unzip the garment.
- Cut and remove the stitches holding the hem, facing, and lining in place over the zipper.
- Cut and remove the stitches holding the zipper in place.
- Clean away all loose threads.
- Separate the two pieces of the new zipper.
- Position the left side of the zipper face down on the left edge of the garment. Push the hem, facing, and lining of the garment out of the way.

- Align the index marks and pin or baste the left side of the zipper in place. Turn the end of the tape under at the top of the zipper, and pin or baste it in place.
- Position the right side of the zipper face down on the right edge of the garment. Push the hem, facing, and lining of the garment out of the way.
- Align the index marks, and pin or baste the right side of the zipper in place. Turn the end of the tape under at the top of the zipper and pin or baste it in place.
- Turn the jacket right side out.
- Stitch the left side of the zipper in place. Tack the seam at the beginning and at the end. Use the old seam line as a guide.
- Stitch the right side of the zipper in place. Tack the seam at the beginning and at the end. Use the old seam line as a guide.
- Re-stitch the hem, facing, and lining in place. Make sure they will not catch in the teeth of the zipper when it is opened and closed.

SECTION VII – Replacing Hook & Pile Fastener

4-30. Hook and pile fasteners (Figure 4-13) are used to close openings and to make adjustments in cuffs and waistbands. Each fastener consists of two pieces of tape. One piece is covered with a thick pile of small nylon loops. The other piece is covered with rows of small nylon hooks. When the two pieces are overlapped and pressed together, the hooks grip the loops. The two pieces will cling together until they are pulled apart. Repeated use can pull out the stitches which were used to attach the fastener to the garment or textile item. The fastener may also lose its clinging ability if lint and debris get caught in the hooks and loops.

Editor's note: *Hook & pile Fasteners are known by everybody but the military as Velcro®*

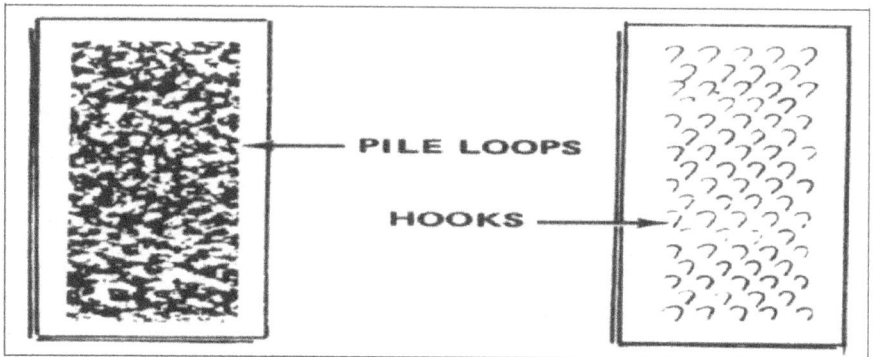

Figure 4-13. Hook and pile fastener

SECTION VIII – Replacing Drawstrings

4-31. Drawstrings are cotton or nylon cords enclosed in casings. Drawstrings are used to make formfitting adjustments in cuffs, waistbands, hoods,

55

and hems. Drawstrings are also used to close openings in textile items such as barracks bags. Drawstrings fray and break with repeated use and washing. They also come out of their casings if they have not been properly secured. To replace a drawstring (Figure 4-14)—

- Remove the stitching that secures the drawstring midway in the casing.
- Untie or cut off the knots in the ends of the drawstring.
- Remove the defective drawstring by pulling it out of one end of the casing.
- Re-stitch both eyelets or replace the metal rings in the casing, if necessary. See page 58 for directions on replacing eyelets.
- Cut a new drawstring the length of the casing plus enough for an extension on each end. (See the specifications on each garment for the exact length of the drawstring.)
- Dip the ends of the drawstring in a synthetic resin or a mixture of 50 percent beeswax and 50 percent paraffin to prevent them from fraying.
- Attach a safety pin to one end of the drawstring to guide the drawstring through the casing.
- Remove the safety pin.
- Even up the ends of the drawstring. Stitch through the casing and the drawstring midway in the casing to anchor the drawstring in place.
- Knot the ends of the drawstring to prevent them from being pulled back through the eyelet into the casing.

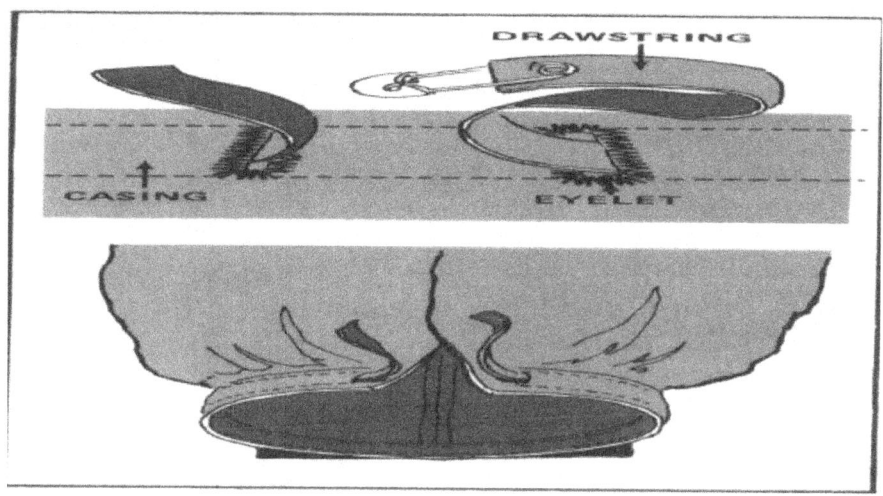

Figure 4-14. Replacing a drawstring

SECTION IX – Replacing Buckles

4-32. The military uses three kinds of buckles on clothing and textile items. One kind consists of a D-ring with a tongue. A belt or strap with a tongued buckle attached to one end is fastened by passing the loose end through the buckle and inserting the tongue into an eyelet. The second kind is a slide buckle with three parallel bars. A belt or strap with this kind of buckle attached to one end is fastened by passing the loose end over and under the bars and pulling the end up taut. The third kind is a hook-type fastener. A belt or strap with this kind of buckle is fastened by hooking the attachment at one end over the attachment at the other end. To replace missing, bent, or defective buckles (Figure 4-15)—

- Notice which bar of the slide buckle the belt or strap is lapped over. On some items, it is the center bar. On others, it is one of the end bars.
- Cut through and remove the stitches at the end of the overlap.
- Unfold the under lap and remove the defective buckle.
- Obtain a new or salvaged buckle the same type and size as the defective buckle. If the buckle is missing, check the item specifications for a description of the buckle.
- Pass the end of the belt or strap through the buckle. Insert the tongue of a tongued buckle through the hole in the belt or strap.
- Turn under the raw edge of the belt or strap. Fold the belt or strap under at the buckle.
- Stitch the under lap in place with two rows of stitching 1/16 to ⅛ inch from the edge. Tack all seams.

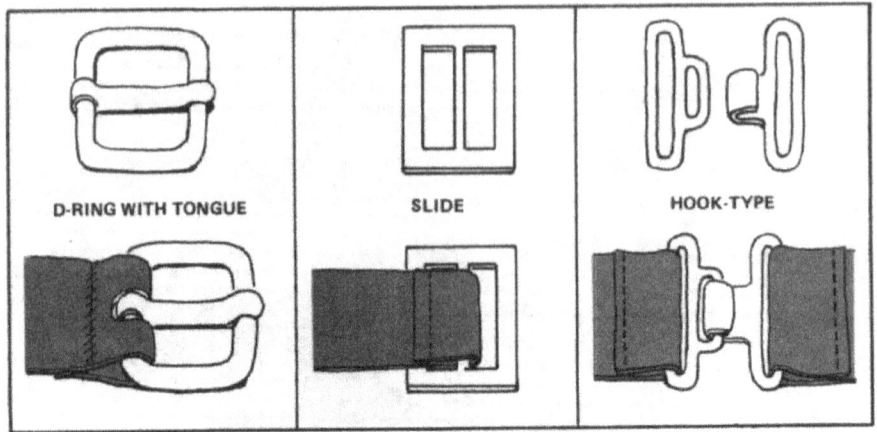

D-RING WITH TONGUE   SLIDE   HOOK-TYPE

Figure 4-15. Replacing a buckle

SECTION X – Repairing or Replacing Eyelets

4-33. Eyelets are used on belts and straps to hold the buckle tongue in place. Eyelets are also used on garments and textile items that have lacing and drawstrings. The edge of an eyelet is reinforced with buttonhole stitches or a metal ring. Most metal eyelets are made of brass. Some are also covered with an enamel finish to match a garment. The stitches sewn around eyelets fray and unravel with repeated use and washing. The metal rings bend, split, and pull away from the surrounding cloth.

Repairing Stitched Eyelets

4-34. To repair stitched eyelets (Figure 4-16)—

- Cut and remove all the buttonhole stitches around the eyelet. Clean away all pieces of thread.
- Close the hole with a reinforced darn.
- Use the appropriate punch on a hole punch to make a new hole for the eyelet.
- Sew buttonhole stitches around the raw edges of the hole.

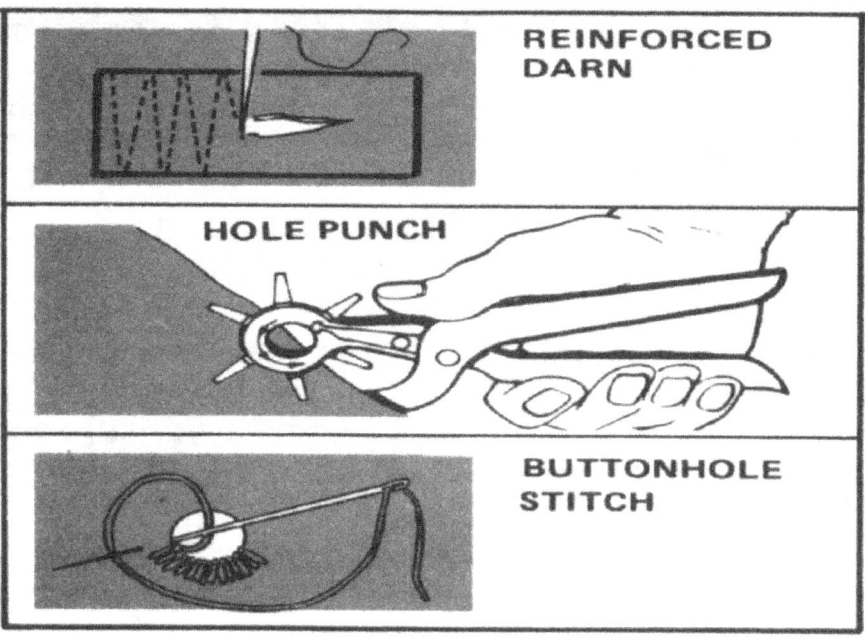

Figure 4-16. Repairing a stitched eyelet

Replacing Metal Eyelets

4-35. To replace metal eyelets (Figure 4-17)—

- Remove the defective eyelet by cutting it out with a pair of wire cutters. Do not cut the surrounding cloth.
- Close the hole with a reinforced darn.
- Obtain an eyelet the same type and color as the one removed.
- Use a hole punch to make a new hole for the eyelet. Make the hole smaller than the eyelet barrel so that the eyelet will fit tightly.
- Turn the cloth face down. Insert the barrel of the eyelet down into the hole.
- Place the washer on the awl.
- Place the cloth face down on the awl so that the barrel of the eyelet rests on the awl.
- Position the eyelets set on the eyelet, and hold it in place.
- Hit the top of the eyelet set with a mallet to set the eyelet in the cloth.

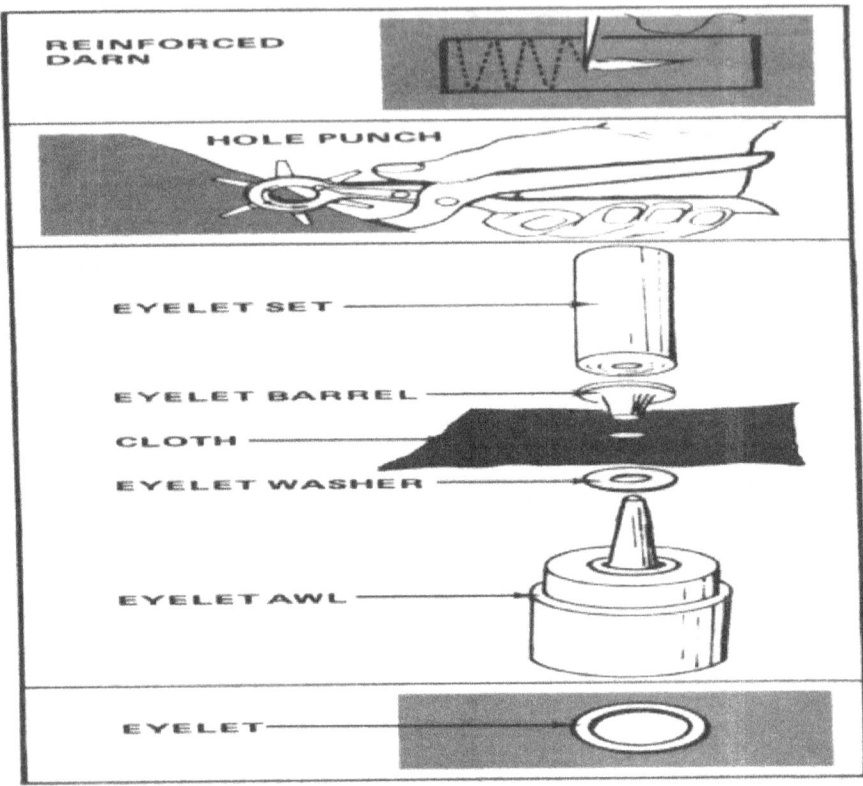

Figure 4-17. Replacing a metal eyelet

SECTION XI – Replacing Snap Fasteners

4-36. Snap fasteners are used in place of buttons. A snap fastener has a male half and a female half. The two halves close under pressure and remain clinched until they are pulled apart. Repeated use and washing damage parts of a snap fastener. The metal pieces bend and split. The surrounding fabric often gives way first, and half of the snap fastener is pulled out of the cloth. To replace a defective snap fastener (Figure 4-18)—

- Place the defective garment or item on a hard surface.
- Remove the two halves. Use wire cutters and a drill, if necessary.
- Close the holes with reinforced darns.
- Use a hole punch to make holes in the darned area. Make the holes smaller than the barrel for the two halves so that the barrels will fit snugly into the holes.
- The female half consists of a cap and a socket. Turn the overlapping cloth face up, and insert the barrel of the cap into the hole.
- Position the cloth face down on the female anvil. Adjust the cloth so that the cap is in the cavity of the anvil.

60

- Place the socket over the barrel with the wide part facing up.
- Insert the set into the barrel, and hold it in place.
- Hit the top of the set with a mallet to set the female half of the snap fastener in the overlapping cloth.
- The male half consists of a post and a stud. Turn the under lapping cloth face down and insert the barrel of the post into the hole.
- Position the cloth face up on the male anvil. Adjust the cloth so that the post is in the ring at the center of the anvil.
- Place the stud over the barrel with the wide part facing down.
- Insert the set into the barrel, and hold it in place.
- Hit the top of the set with a mallet to set the male half of the snap fastener in the under lapping cloth.

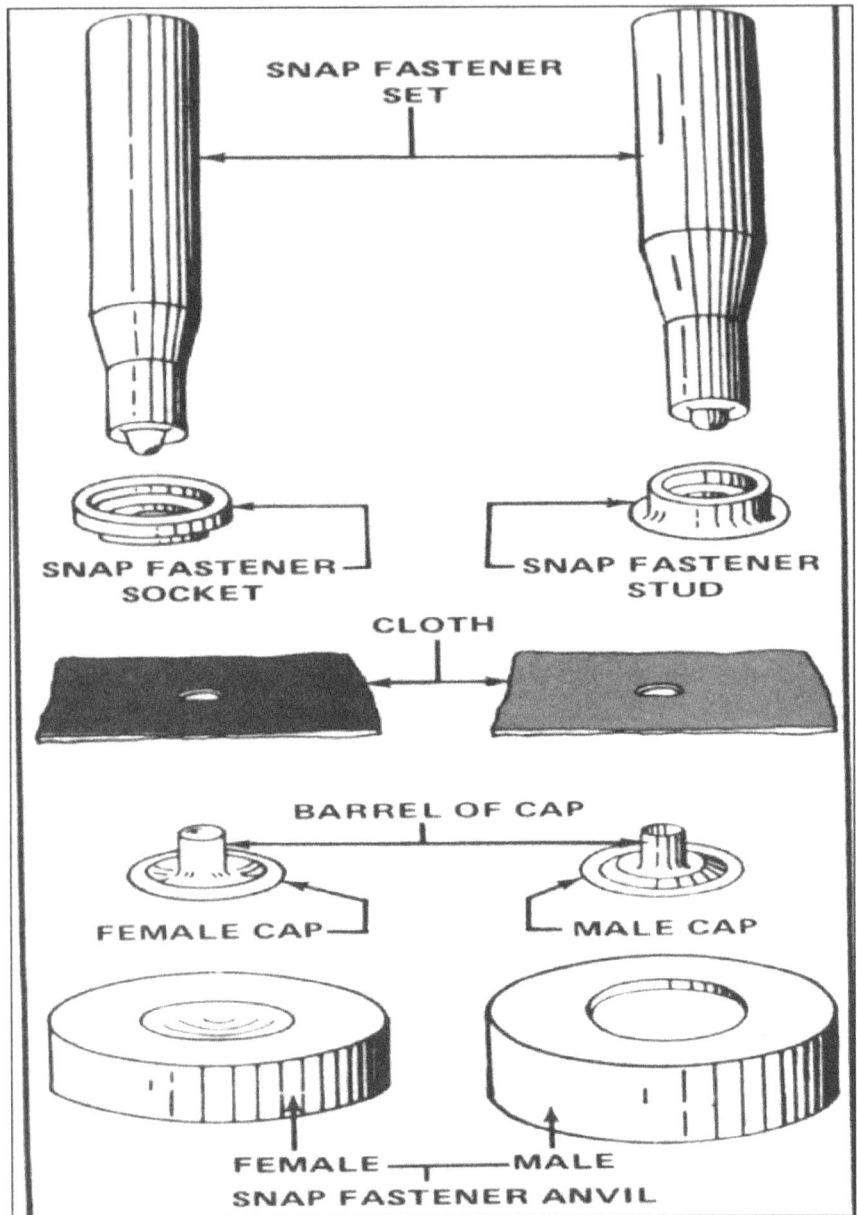

Figure 4-18. Replacing a snap fastener

SECTION XII – Stitching Bindings

4-37. A binding is a woven cloth tape used to enclose the raw edges of fabric that is too thick to fold and hem. Fabric repair specialists replace worn, torn, or loose bindings. They also use bindings to reinforce the frayed edges of cuffs and hems. Some sewing machines have binding attachments that fold and guide the binding during sewing. The instructions for using attachments are in the technical manual for the sewing machine. A binding can also be sewn on without using a binding attachment.

SECTION XIII – Repairing Open Seams

4-38. An open seam is a seam with broken and missing threads. Open and defective seams are repaired by re-stitching. All re-stitching is done by machine, except in an emergency. Well-done re-stitching matches the original stitching closely. The color and type of thread and the type of seam used to construct the garment or textile item. The size of the stitches matches that of the original stitches on either side of the repair. All loose threads are cleaned away. Re-stitching overlaps the original stitching by at least ½ inch at both ends. All seams are tacked at both ends to prevent unraveling.

Section XIV – Replacing Collars

4-39. Some clothing is received in clothing repair shops with frayed collars. The rest of these garments may show little wear. The ragged collars take away from the neat appearance of the garments. If the damaged collars are replaced, the garments can be reissued. Instructions given here are general directions for replacing a collar using seam type 5. The collars on military shirts, coats, and jackets differ. It may be necessary to modify these instructions to repair a specific garment. To replace a collar (Figure 4-19)—

- Remove the defective collar by cutting through all the stitches holding it in place. Do not cut or damage the cloth in the rest of the garment. Clean away all loose threads.
- Place the back of the garment face up on a worktable.
- Mark a chalk line around the neck of the garment ½ inch from the raw edge.
- Obtain a matching replacement collar. Use a collar salvaged from a similar garment that has been scrapped or make one from cloth using the old collar as a pattern. Match the fabric fading as closely as possible.
- Center the collar face up on the neck of the garment.
- Separate the two layers of the collar.
- Sew the bottom layer to the neck of the garment along the chalk line. Tack the seam at each end.
- Turn the garment inside out and turn the collar up.
- Press the seam allowances of the neck and bottom layer to the inside of the collar.
- Fold the seam allowance of the top layer of the collar to the inside and press the folded edge in place.
- Position the fold so that it overlaps the previous seam line by ⅛ inch.

- Sew a row of stitches 1/16 inch from the folded edge. Tack the seam at each end.

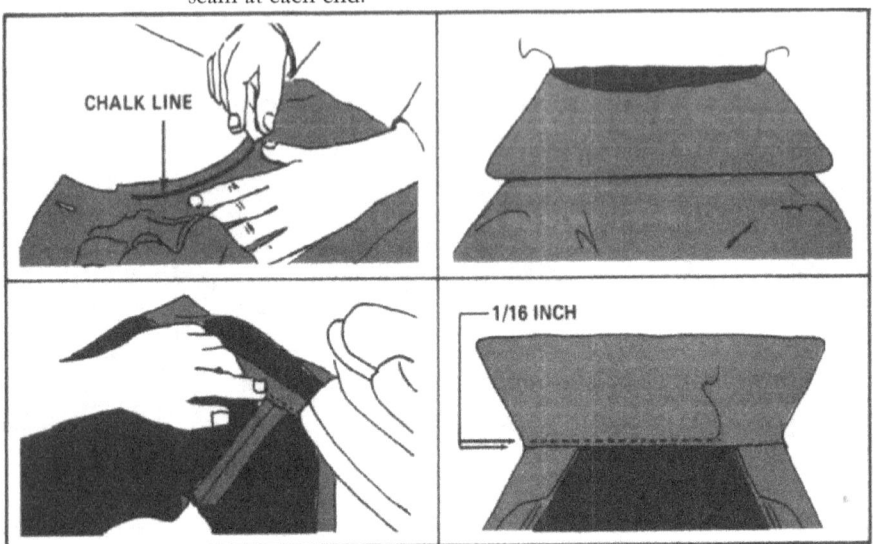

Figure 4-19. Replacing a collar

SECTION XV – Replacing Patch Pockets, Pockets Flaps, & Belt Loops

4-40. Patch pockets are sewn to a garment by stitching around all sides of the pockets except the top. Pocket flaps are attached to garments by stitching on edge of the flaps a little above the pocket tops. They give a tailored look to pockets and are used to close pockets securely. Loops are usually attached to a garment at the waistband or collar edge. They are used to hold a belt in place or to hang the garment on a hook. All of these cloth attachments are subject to wear and tear. They are pulled loose from garments. The cloth frays and the stitches unravel. Items turned in for repair with loose, worn, torn, or missing cloth attachments are restored as nearly as possible to their original appearance. Frayed or missing items are replaced with salvaged or tailor-made ones. Loose items are securely re-stitched. Directions are given here for attaching a patch pocket, a pocket flap, and a belt loop.

Replacing a Patch Pocket

4-41. To replace a patch pocket (Figure 4-20)—
Remove the damaged pocket by cutting through all the stitches holding it in place. Do not cut the underlying fabric of the garment. Clean away all loose threads. Place the garment face up on the worktable.

- Obtain a matching replacement pocket. Use one salvaged from a similar garment that has been scrapped or make one from cloth using the old pocket as a pattern. Match the fabric fading as closely as possible.

64

- Place the new pocket face up on top of the garment. Cover the same area that the old pocket covered. Pin the pocket in place.
- Measure and mark a chalk line ¼ inch from the folded edge on all sides of the pocket except the top.
- Position the pocket and the garment under the needle of the sewing machine.
- Stick the needle into the pocket 1/16 inch down from the right side of the pocket.
- Stitch down 1 inch and then back up to the starting point to tack the seam.
- Pivot the cloth on the needle, and take one or two stitches to the chalk line.
- Pivot the cloth on the needle, and stitch around the pocket on the chalk line. Pivot the cloth on the needle at the corners.
- Pivot the cloth on the needle 1/16 inch away from the top edge of the cloth. Take one or two stitches so that the needle is now 1/16 inch away from the side of the pocket.
- Pivot the cloth on the needle again, and stitch down 1 inch and then back up 1 inch to tack the seam.

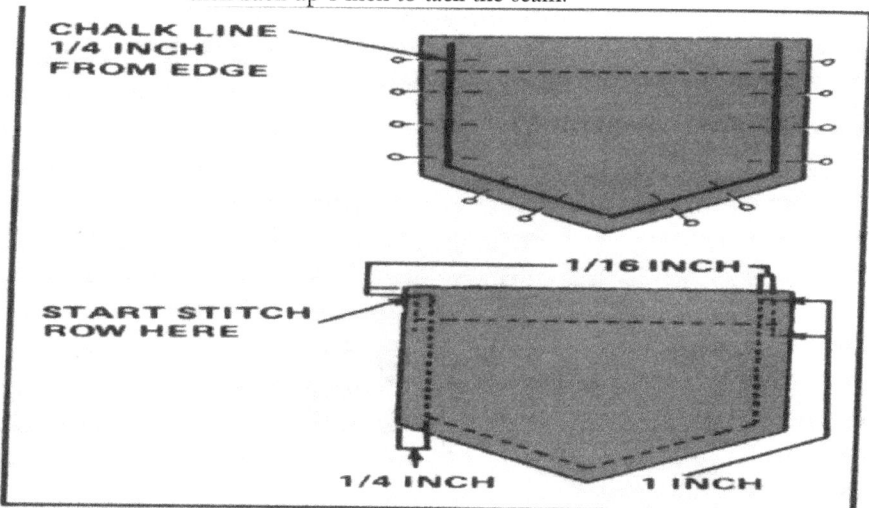

Figure 4-20. Replacing a patch pocket

Replacing a Pocket Flap

4-42. To replace a pocket flap (Figure 4-21)—

- Remove the damaged pocket flap by cutting through all the stitches holding it in place. Do not cut the underlying fabric of the garment. Clean away all loose threads. Place the garment face up on the worktable.

65

- Obtain a matching replacement pocket flap. Use one salvaged from a similar garment that has been scrapped or make one from cloth using the old pocket flap as a pattern. Match the fabric fading as closely as possible.
- Measure and mark a chalk line on both sides of the pocket ½ inch from the raw edge at the top of the pocket flap.
- Cut ½ inch off the top of the bottom layer of the pocket flap. Use the chalk line as a cutting guide.
- Fold under the top layer of the pocket flap ½ inch. Use the chalk line as a guide. Press the folded edge flat.
- Place the pocket flap face up ½ inch above the pocket.
- Make a row of stitches ¼ inch from the folded edge. Tack the seam 1 inch at each end.

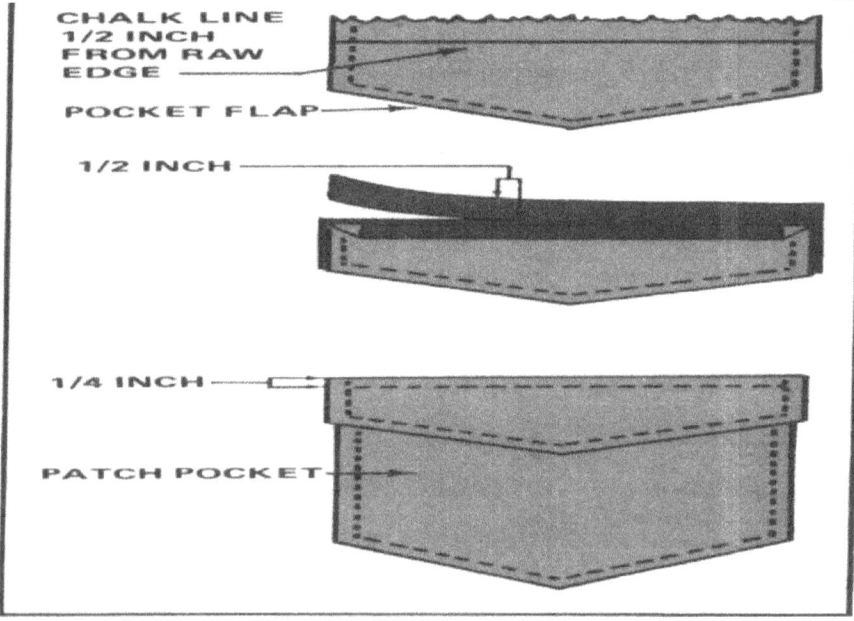

CHALK LINE 1/2 INCH FROM RAW EDGE

POCKET FLAP

1/2 INCH

1/4 INCH

PATCH POCKET

Figure 4-21. Attaching a pocket flap

Replacing a Belt Loop

4-43. To replace a belt loop--
- Remove the damaged belt loop by cutting through all the stitches holding it in place. Do not cut the underlying fabric. Clean away all loose threads. Position the garment face up under the needle of the sewing machine.
- Obtain a matching belt loop. Use one salvaged from a similar garment that has been scrapped or make one from cloth using the old belt loop as a pattern. Match fabric fading as closely as possible.

- Put the belt loop face down on the waistband where the old belt loop was located. Overlap the top of the waistband by ½ inch.
- Stitch across the belt loop ¼ inch from the top of the waistband. Tack the seam.
- Bring the free end of the belt loop over the waistband and turn it under ¼ inch.
- Lay the belt loop flat against the garment.
- Stitch across the belt loop ⅛ inch from the folded edge. Tack the seam.

CHAPTER 5 - INSPECTING AND MARKING CANVAS AND WEBBING

SECTION I – Initial Inspections

5-1. Defective canvas and webbed items are initially inspected to determine whether or not they can be repaired economically. Items not worth repairing are set aside to be cannibalized later for usable parts and cloth. Defects that can be repaired at a reasonable cost are marked with white chalk. Figure 5-1 gives the seven symbols to be used during the inspection of canvas and webbing items. When defective canvas and webbed items are received in a fabric repair shop, they are first tested for fabric strength. Fabric strength is the ability of the cloth to resist tearing. It is tested by folding the cloth on the straight grain, grasping a small section of the fold between the thumb and the forefinger of each hand, gripping it so that the fingers touch, and tugging firmly on the cloth several times. If the cloth does not rip, it is strong enough to be used again. If the cloth rips, several other sections are tested to determine their strength. If they rip, the item is set aside to salvage the usable hardware. Items that pass the fabric strength test are then inspected for other defects. After tents and other heavy items have passed the fabric strength test, they are hoisted by a block and tackle and inspected section by section from the top down.

5-2. Tents are raised a few feet at a time. An inspector examines each newly exposed area on the inside and points out the defects to another inspector who marks the defects on the outside surface with chalk.

Table 5-1 lists the areas marked by the inspector.

SECTION II –Final Inspections

5-3. After canvas and webbed items are repaired, they are re-inspected. These inspections are made to make sure that all repairs were done properly and that no defects were missed by either the initial inspector or the fabric repair specialist. Each repair is closely examined to determine if the correct thread, stitch length, and seam type were used. All breaks in stitching are checked for backstitching. Patches are inspected to make sure they match the fabric of the canvas item in weight and color. Repairs to webbed items are examined to determine if the correct size webbing was used and if the repairs were stitched properly. Replaced hardware is checked to make sure it is installed correctly. All detachable items, such as liners and sashes, are examined to make sure they were repaired and reattached to the right tent.

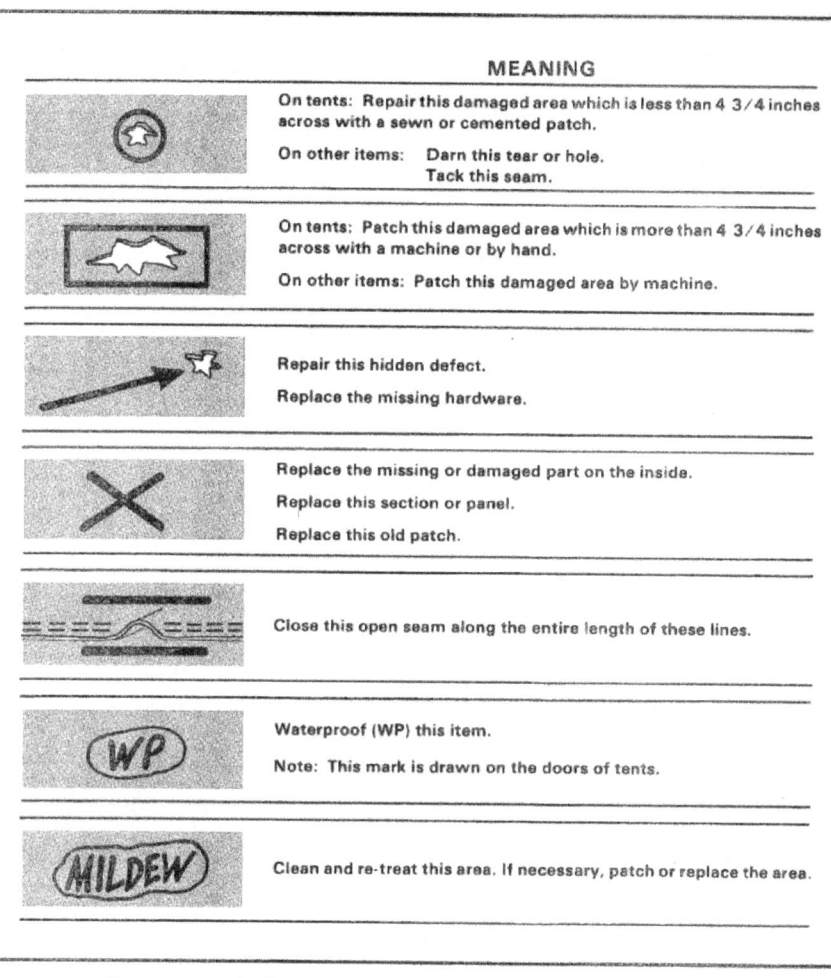

Figure 5-1. Chalk marks used on canvas and webbed items
Inspecting and Marking Canvas and Webbing

69

Defect	Repair
Canvas:	
Worn or weak areas (Worn areas are usually located where the canvas rubs against other objects. Weak areas are those that fail the strength test.)	Replace or patch
Holes (Chalk marks is placed next to the hole.)	Patch
Area with several holes	Replace
Tears	Darn or patch
Mildew-stained areas	Clean and re-treat
Overly patched areas	Replace
Badly repaired areas	Repair again
Broken threads	Restitch
Open seams	Restitch
Poorly sewn seams in which the stitches run off the edge of the cloth	Restitch
Seams in which the thread has rotted	Restitch
Soiled areas (Fading is acceptable and so are spots and stains that remain in the canvas after it has been cleaned.)	Clean and re-treat
Webbing:	
Frayed ends	Repair
Broken or loose stitching	Restitch
Worn, torn, or damaged webbing	Replace
Mildew-stained webbing	Clean and re-treat
Mildew-rotted webbing	Replace
Hardware:	
Rusty, bent, broken, or cracked hardware	Replace
Missing hardware (Chalk mark points to the spot where the replacement hardware should be attached.)	Replace
Electro-zinc-plated hardware which has a dull, flaky finish	Replace with hot-galvanized finished hardware which has a bright smooth finish
Lines:	
Frayed ends	Repair
Weak, worn, or broken lines	Replace
Loose splicing	Re-splice
Mildew-stained lines	Clean and re-treat
Mildew-rotted lines	Replace
Excessively stretched lines	Shorten or replace
Special items and attachments:	
Ventilator opening or cover with more than two patches or defects	Replace
Ventilator duct with a hole or tear	Patch with either cemented or sew patch

Table 5-1. Areas marked in initial inspection of canvas and webbing

Blackout patch which does not close properly and allows light to shine through the gap	Replace
Improperly sized window flap	Replace
Extension cloth which causes the tent to wrinkle	Replace
Defective window frame assembly	Repair with a patch that does not distort the window opening
Window sash made of cellulose acetate and cotton netting	Replace with a flexible waterproof film sash
Exposed needle holes around previously replaced sash products	Replace sash pocket with a larger sash pocket that covers the holes
Defective outlet sash	Repair or patch if the repair sash and if no more than three patches will be used

Table 5-1. Areas marked in initial inspection of canvas and webbing

CHAPTER 6 - USING THE TENTAGE REPAIR KIT

SECTION I – Components of the Kit

6-1. Repairs to canvas and webbing are made using a sewing machine when possible. Occasionally, it is necessary to repair a tent by hand. Hand repairs to canvas and webbing require special tools, which are part of the tentage repair kit. The kit also contains the cloth and replacement parts necessary to repair a tent.

When completely stocked with all 24 items, the kit measures 16 by 16 by 12 inches and weighs 30 ½ pounds. Figure 6-1 shows the components of the kit. Table 6-1 describes each item and lists the national stock number used to order replacements. Fabric repair specialists are responsible for restocking the kit.

SECTION II – Care of Tools

6-2. Fabric repair specialists are responsible for taking care of the tools in tentage repair kits. They check tools periodically and perform maintenance as needed. Needles are kept dry and free of rust. Blunt needles are replaced. Saddle soap is used to keep sewing palms soft and flexible. The sewing palms must be kept dry so that the metal inset does not rust. Cutting punches are used only on wood or lead blocks to keep the edges from becoming dull. The hollow areas in cutting punches are cleaned out regularly so that they do not become packed with bits of cloth. Punch and die sets are kept clean. They are stored in a dry place or lightly coated with oil to prevent rust. Steel hammers are never used on cutting punches or punch and die sets because they strike too severe a blow. Their use could damage the tools and could cause metal pieces to chip off and hit someone in the eye. Rawhide mallets are checked for cracks in the handle and in the rawhide. They are never used to drive nails or anything else that could cut through the rawhide. Shears are kept clean and sharp. They are never used for any purpose other than to cut cloth and thread. The saddler's sewing awl is kept clean. Wire brushes are cleaned after use. The bristles are kept dry to prevent rust.

1 ADHESIVE	2 AWL	3 BRUSH	4 CASE
5 CLOTH	6 FM 10-16	7 SIZE 4 GROMMETS	8 SIZE 5 GROMMETS
9 SLIDE FASTENER LUBRICANT	10 RAWHIDE MALLET	11 SAILMAKER'S NEEDLES	12 SEWING PALM
13 SIZE 5 CUTTING PUNCH	14 SIZE 6 CUTTING PUNCH	15 CONNECTING RINGS	16 CONNECTING RINGS
17 CONNECTING RINGS	18 SIZE 4 PUNCH AND DIE SET	19 SIZE 5 PUNCH AND DIE SET	20 BENT TRIMMER'S SHEARS
21 SLING			
22 TENT LINE SLIPS		23 THREAD	24 TWINE

Figure 6-1. Components of the tentage repair kit

Component	Description	Number Per Kit	National Stock Number
Adhesive (1)	Canned solution of synthetic rubber which is waterproof, flexible, and very sticky Used to cement patches to canvas	8 tubes	8040-01-033-7507
Awl, saddler's sewing (2)	Pointed, hand-held tool which comes with two straight needles and one curved needle Used to make a lockstitch by hand	1 each	5120-00-257-5541
Brush, wire, scratch (3)	Tool with a hardwood handle and wire bristles Used to clean canvas and webbing	1 each	7920-00-291-5815
Case, tentage repair kit (4)	Canvas carryall with webbed handles and straps which unfolds to reveal two compartments and a number of pockets Used to hold tools, cloth, and repair parts	8 yards	8305-00-926-6171
GSTM 4-42-.21 (6)	Detailed instructions for repairing canvas and webbing Used as a guide by fabric repair specialists	1 each	
Grommet, metallic 0.320-inch, size 4 (7)	Two-part, brass eyelet with a ½ inch inside diameter Used to reinforce areas where holes are made to hold ropes, lines, spindles, and straps	1 gross	5325-00-231-6622
Grommet, metallic, 0.380-inch, size 5 (8)	Two-part, brass eyelet with a ? inch inside diameter Used to reinforce areas where holes are made to hold ropes, lines, spindles, and straps	100 each	5325-00-202-2053
Lubricant, interlocking slide fastener (9)	Stick of wax Used to lubricate the teeth in a zipper	1 box	9150-00-999-7548
Mallet, rawhide (10)	Hammer with a wooden handle and a leather head Used to hit dies and punches	1 each	5120-00-222-2200
Needle, sailmaker's, size 14 (11)	Slender, pointed sewing instrument Used to hand sew on canvas	1 package	8315-00-163-1547
Palm, sewing	Leather shield worn over the palm which has a metal inset that forces needle through canvas and webbing Used to protect the palm during sewing	1 each	5120-00-223-6838
Punch, cutting, size 5 (13)	Tool with a sharp, circular end ½-inch in diameter Used to cut grommet holes	1 each	5110-00-180-0923

Table 6-1. Data on tentage repair kit

CHAPTER 7 - HAND SEWING ON CANVAS AND WEBBING

SECTION I – Hand Sewing

7-1. Repairs on canvas and webbing are made by hand sewing only when it is not possible to use a sewing machine. Hand sewing is used when electrical power is not available. It is used when the canvas or webbed item is too bulky to fit under the needle of the sewing machine or when repairs are made on a tent that is set up.

SECTION II – Sailmaker's Needle

7-2. A sailmaker's needle (Figure 7-1) is designed to penetrate thick canvas. It has a triangular shape that tapers to a sharp point at one end and rounds off and has a large eye at the other end. It is used to make all the hand-sewn stitches used on canvas except the lockstitch. Certain preparations must be made before a sailmaker's needle is used to repair canvas or webbing.

Estimate the Amount Thread

7-3. The fabric repair specialist estimates how much thread will be needed to complete a repair by first determining how many strands of thread should be used. The weight of the cloth and the type of the repair determine the strands to use. Very heavy canvas and areas that get a lot of stress are repaired with four strands of thread instead of two strands to add strength to the repair. To estimate how much thread is needed to make a repair, measure the damage and determine the total length of the repair seam. Cut the thread as follows:

- Two-Strand Thread. Measure and cut a piece of thread six times longer than the total length of the repair seam.
- Four-Strand Thread. Measure and cut a piece of thread 12 times longer than the total length of the repair seam.

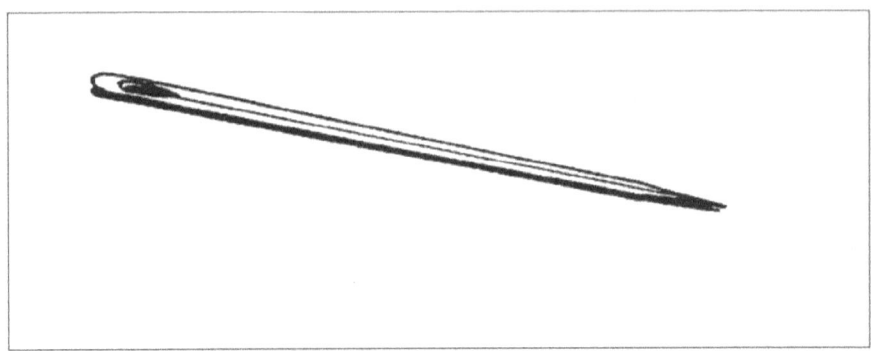

Figure 7-1. Sailmaker's needle

Waxing the Thread

7-4. The fabric repair specialist uses technical beeswax (NSN 9160-00-253-1173) to wax the piece of thread to keep it from fraying and to protect it from mildew and the weather. Waxing the thread helps the thread to pass more easily through the hole made by the sailmaker's needle. To wax a piece of thread (Figure 7-2)--

- Hold one end of the thread against the piece of beeswax with the thumb of one hand.
- Grasp the thread, and pull the entire length of the thread across the surface of the beeswax with the other hand.
- Repeat these steps until the thread is sticky.

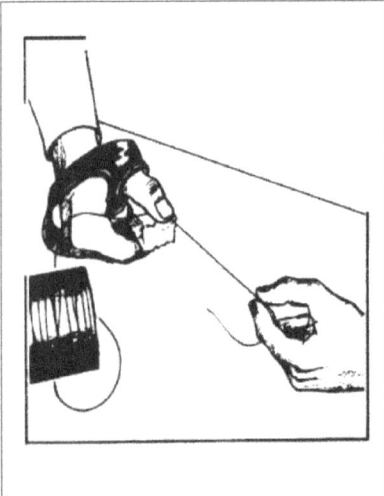
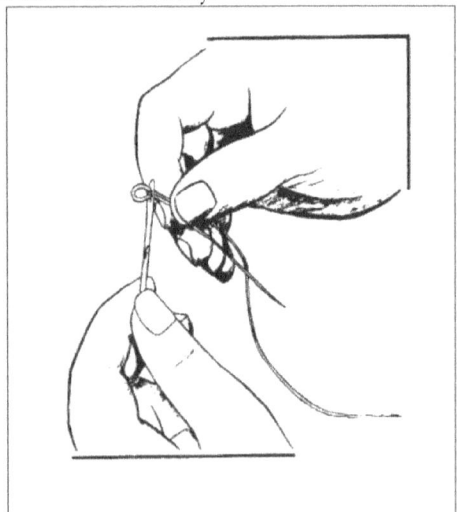

Figure 7-2. Waxing the thread and threading a sailmaker's needle

Threading the Needle

7-5. The fabric repair specialist threads the needle with waxed thread. To thread a sailmaker's needle (Figure 7-2)--

- Fold over the piece of thread to form a small loop. Make the loop near one end of the thread if two strands are used. Make the loop at a point halfway between the ends if four strands are used.
- Stick the loop through the eye of the needle.
- Pull half of the thread through the eye and make the ends even.
- Tie the ends in a knot.

Re-waxing the Thread

7-6. The fabric repair specialist re-waxes the thread for added protection. To re-wax the thread (Figure 7-3)--

- Hold the thread near the needle firmly with one hand.
- Grasp a section of thread with the fingertips of the other hand and twist the strands together.
- Rub this section across the surface of the beeswax.
- Repeat these steps until the entire length of the thread has been re-waxed.

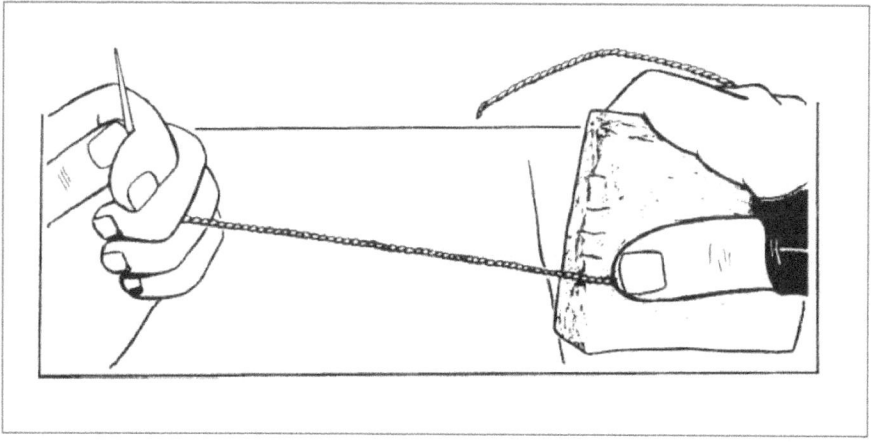

Figure 7-3. Re-waxing thread

Putting on the Sewing Palm

7-7. The fabric repair specialist wears a sewing palm to protect the hand while sewing with the sailmaker's needle. The palm has a metal inset which is used to push the needle through canvas or webbing. To put on a sewing palm (Figure 7-4)--

- Grasp the sewing palm with the left hand so that the smaller (thumb) opening is on the right and the metal inset is facing up.
- Turn the right hand so that the palm is facing up.
- Slip the four fingers of the right hand through the larger opening and slip the thumb through the smaller opening.

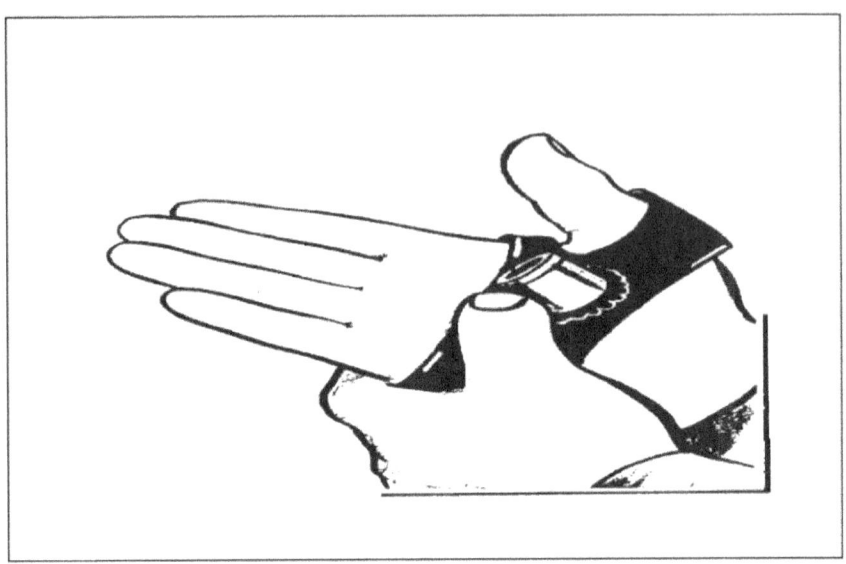

Figure 7-4. Putting on a sewing palm

Note: These instructions are for a right-handed person. A left-handed person should get a sewing palm designed to be worn on the left hand and should change left to right and right to left in the instructions above.

SECTION III – Saddler's Sewing Awl

7-8. The saddler's sewing awl (Figure 7-5) is a sewing tool designed to make a lockstitch by hand. It has a bulb-shaped, wooden handle which holds a bobbin and extra needles. The bobbin feeds waxed thread to a needle attached to the tapered end of the handle. The sewing awl is equipped with two straight needles and one curved needle. The straight needles are used to make repairs in flat areas where there is plenty of room to work. The curved needle is used in areas where there is little room in which to work with the awl, such as inside corners. To thread a sewing awl—

- Remove the bobbin cap and take out the bobbin. If necessary, refill the metal bobbin by wrapping waxed thread around it.
- Unwind 6 inches of thread and stick the end of the thread inside the handle. Pull it out through the hole in the side of the handle.
- Put the bobbin back inside the handle and replace the bobbin cap.
- Pull the thread down the handle and wrap it around the tension post one time. Pass the end of the thread under the thread coming out of the hole so that the thread will feed freely. See the inset on Figure 7-6.
- Unscrew and remove the chuck cap.
- Stick the end of the thread in the groove beside the tension post and pass the end of the thread through the hole in the metal cap.
- Stick the needle into the chuck so that the groove in the needle is aligned with the groove in the handle.

- Thread the needle.
- Stick the end of the thread through the chuck cap and then pass the chuck cap over the needle.
- Screw the cap tightly on the chuck to hold the needle in place. Do not catch the end of the thread inside the chuck cap.

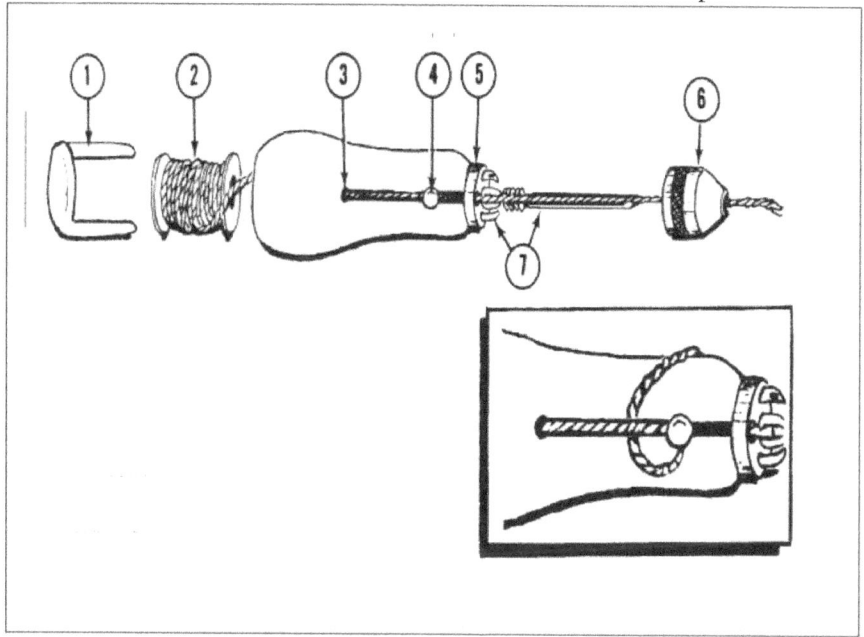

Figure 7-5. Threading saddler's sewing awl

SECTION IV – Hand Stitches

7-9. There are six hand stitches used to repair canvas and webbing when machine repairs are not possible. Three of these stitches are also used to repair clothing. They are the running stitch, the backstitch, and the felling stitch. The round stitch and the fishbone stitch are used in the repair of canvas and webbing only. The lockstitch, made by hand using a sewing awl, is identical to the stitch made by a sewing machine.

Running Stitch

7-10. The running stitch (Figure 7-6), is also called the flat stitch in canvas repair. It is used to hold two pieces of canvas or webbing together until machine repairs can be made. To make a row of running stitches--

- Push the sailmaker's needle through the canvas or webbing and pull the thread through to the knot.
- Backstitch to tack the beginning of the row. See paragraph below.
- Push the needle down through the canvas or webbing and then up through the canvas or webbing.

- Continue to make one or two stitches at a time to the end of the row. Make the stitches uniform in appearance and the same distance apart. Do not try to weave the needle in and out several times because the canvas and webbing are too thick and stiff.
- Backstitch to tack the end of the row.
- Make a knot in the thread close to the canvas and cut off the remaining thread.

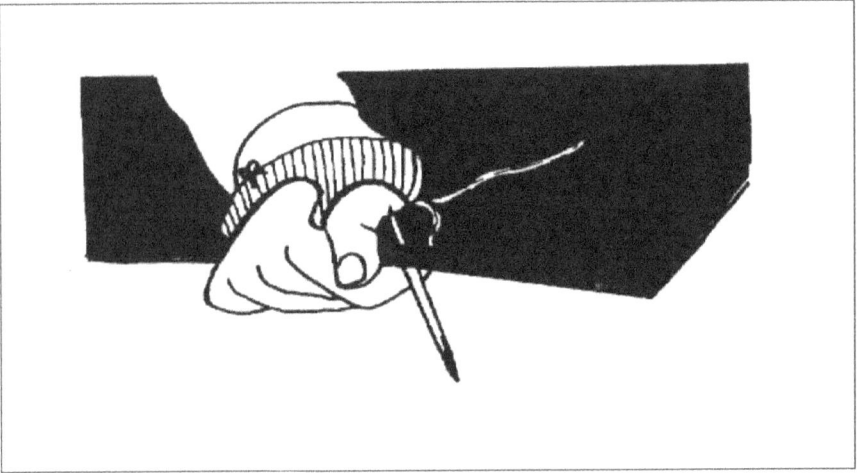

Figure 7-6. Running stitch on canvas

Backstitch

7-11. The backstitch (Figure 7-7) is used on canvas to close an open seam and to tack the beginning and the end of a row of hand stitches. To make a row of backstitches--

- Push the sailmaker's needle through the canvas or webbing, and pull the thread through to the knot.
- Tack the beginning of the row by tacking two small stitches, one on top of the other.
- Push the needle up through the canvas or webbing one stitch length from the first two stitches.
- Take one stitch back, pushing the needle down into the canvas or webbing at the end of the first two stitches.
- Push the needle up through the canvas or webbing one stitch length in front of the previous stitch.
- Stitch back, pushing the needle down into the canvas or webbing at the end of the previous stitch.
- Continue to stitch to the end of the row as in 5 and 6 above.
- Tack the end of the row by taking two stitches, one on top of the other.

- Make a knot in the thread close to the canvas, and cut off the remaining thread.

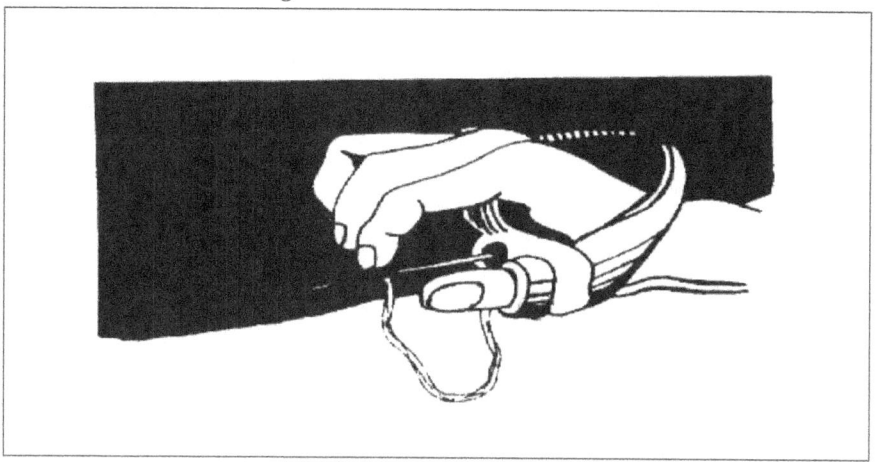

Figure 7-7. Backstitch on canvas

Felling Stitch

7-12. The felling stitch (Figure 7-8) is also called the overhand stitch in canvas repair. It is used to attach a patch by hand. To make a row of felling stitches--

- Push the sailmaker's needle through the canvas, and pull the thread through the canvas to the knot.
- Backstitch to tack the beginning of the row.
- Push the needle down vertically into the canvas at a point that is just beyond the folded edge of the patch.
- Push the needle back up through the canvas and the patch at a diagonal angle.
- Continue to take first a vertical stitch on top and then a diagonal stitch underneath until the repair is complete.
- Backstitch to tack the row of stitches at the end.
- Make a knot in the thread close to the canvas, and cut off the remaining thread.

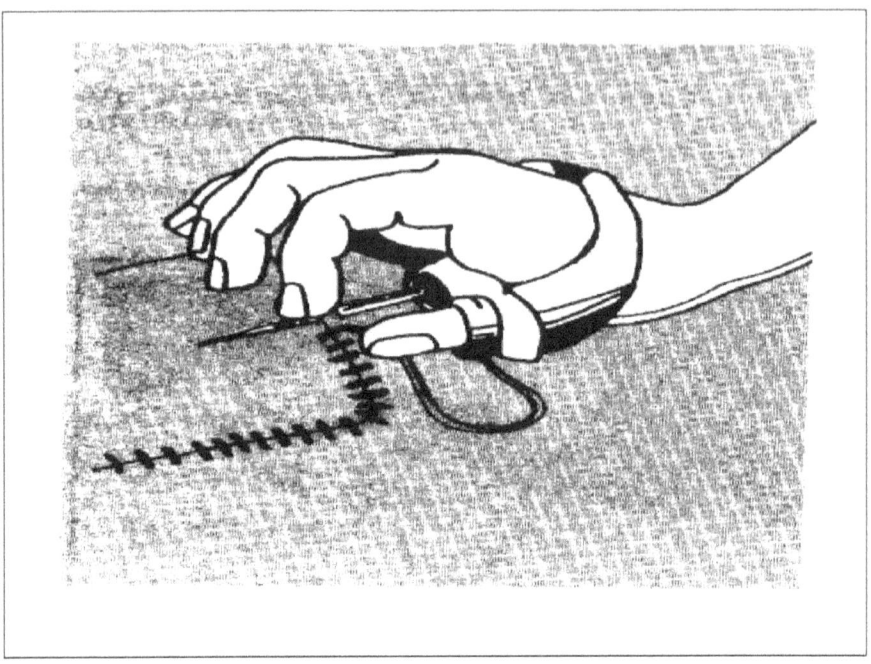

Figure 7-8. Felling stitch on canvas

Round Stitch

7-13. The round stitch (Figure 7-9) is used to hand sew a grommet in place. To make a row of round stitches--

- Thread the sailmaker's needle but do not tie the ends in a knot.
- Push the needle down through the canvas and draw the thread through the canvas until a ½ inch end is left.
- Bring the thread and needle around the edge of the canvas and cross over the ½ inch end.
- Push the needle down through the canvas again.
- Continue wrapping the thread around the edge and sticking the needle down into the canvas to cover the ½ inch end.
- At the end of the row of stitches, stick the needle under a ½ inch section of stitches and pull the thread through to cover the end. Cut off the remaining thread.

Figure 7-9. Round stitch

Fishbone Stitch

7-14. The fishbone stitch (Figure 7-10) is also called the baseball stitch. It is used to join the edges of a tear until the area can be patched. To make a row of fishbone stitches--

- Push the needle up through the canvas. Anchor the knot by taking two stitches, one on top of the other as shown.
- After taking the second stitch, bring the needle and thread up through the opening diagonally.
- Stick the needle down into the canvas on the opposite side of the opening.
- Continue to make diagonal stitches, coming up through the opening and alternating from one side to the other with the stitches.
- End the row by taking two stitches, one on top of the other.
- Make a knot in the thread close to the canvas, and cut off the remaining thread.

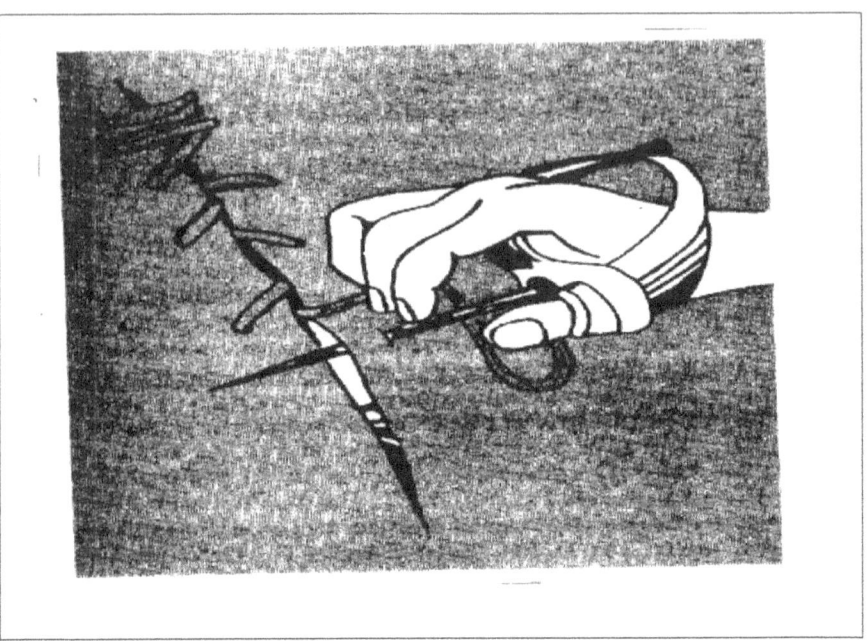

Figure 7-10. Fishbone stitch

Lockstitch

7-15. The lockstitch (Figure 7-11) is used to hand stitch extra-heavy canvas or several thicknesses of canvas together permanently. To make a row of lockstitches-

- Thread a saddler's sewing awl, leaving ½ inch of thread sticking out of the needle.
- Grasp the thread where it comes out of the hole in the handle. Pull enough thread out of the hole to reach from the beginning to the end of the area to be repaired.

Note: This thread is the bottom thread for the lockstitch row.

- Stick the needle down into the cloth at the beginning of the proposed stitch line.
- With the needle still down in the cloth, grasp the end of the thread in the needle. Pull until all the slack thread has been drawn through the eye of the needle to the underside of the cloth.
- Grasping the slack thread so that it cannot be pulled back through the cloth, pull the needle out of the cloth.
- Stick the needle down into the cloth, a stitch length away from the first hole.
- Pull the needle out halfway, forming a loop on the underside with the thread.

- Stick the end of the slack thread through the loop and pull all the slack thread through the loop.
- Grasp the slack thread firmly.
- Pull the needle all the way out of the cloth.
- Pull on the handle and the slack thread equally hard to tighten the stitch and to center the lock in the cloth.

Note: Pulling too hard on the handle causes the stitch to lock on top of the cloth. Not pulling hard enough on the handle causes the stitch to lock on the underside of the cloth. Equal tension on both threads results in a stitch correctly locked halfway between the top and the bottom.

- Before taking each new stitch, pull 2 to 3 inches of thread from the bobbin.
- Continue stitching to the end of the row.
- Finish stitching by cutting the loop formed on the last stitch and tying the two loose ends on the underside in a square knot.

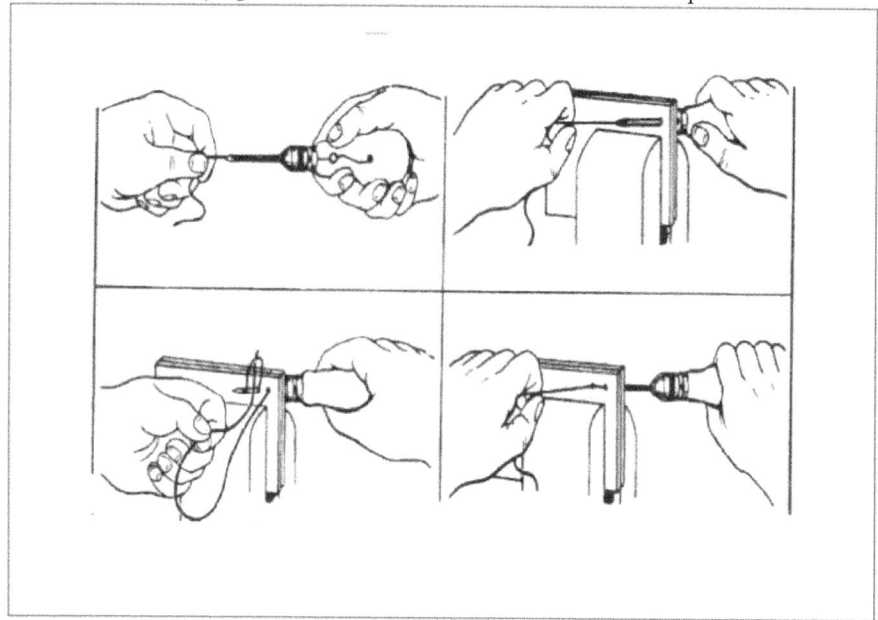

Figure 7-11. Lockstitch made with saddler's sewing awl

CHAPTER 8 - MACHINE SEWING ON CANVAS AND WEBBING

SECTION I – Machine Sewing

8-1. Machine sewing on canvas and webbing is preferred to hand sewing. The stitches made by a machine look better and wear longer than those made by hand. Machine sewing also takes less time.

Repairs to canvas and webbing should be made by machine as often as possible.

SECTION II – Sewing Machines, Needles, & Thread

8-2. The military uses single-needle, heavy-duty sewing machines (Figure 8-1) with compound feed and high-lift alternating pressure. The machines are designed for the repair of canvas and tents. Instructions for operating and maintaining the machines can be found in the manufacturer's manuals or the appropriate technical manuals. The information on page 22 through 24 on needles, thread, stitch length, pressure, and tension also applies to the machines used to repair lightweight and heavy canvas. A size 22 needle is used for repairing lightweight canvas and a size 24 needle is used for repairing heavy canvas. Type I or II, class I polyester thread is used for canvas repair. Left-twist thread is used in the needle and right-twist thread is used in the bobbin. Thread sizes E and F are used to repair lightweight canvas and thread size FF is used to repair heavy canvas. Repairs are sewn seven stitches to an inch on lightweight canvas and five stitches to an inch on heavy canvas.

8-3. There are five seams used by the military to repair canvas and webbing. Four seams are similar to those used to repair clothing. They are the plain seam, the hemming seam, the single-felled seam, and the double-felled seam. The other seam is the flat seam. They are used by fabric repair specialists in the repair of canvas and webbing only. The characteristics of a good seam were given on page 28. These high standards also apply to seams sewn on canvas and webbing.

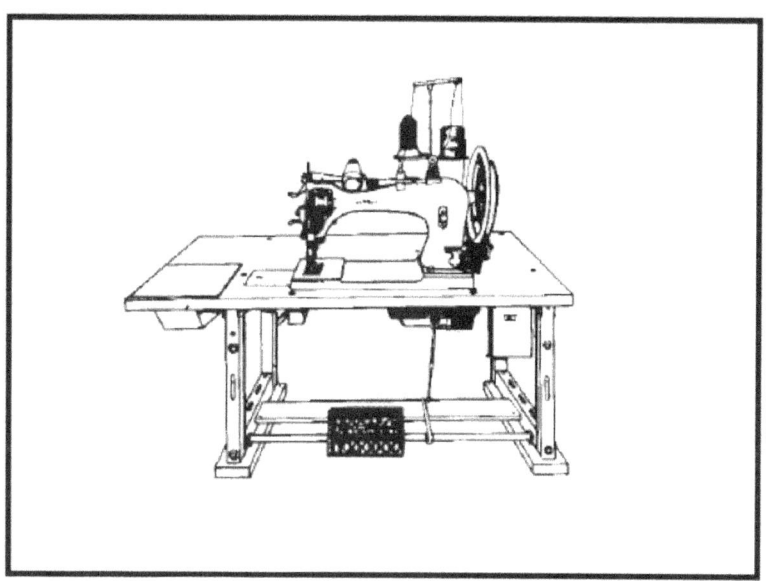

Figure 8-1. Heavy-duty sewing machine

Plain or Simple Seam

8-4. The plain seam (Figure 8-2) is used to join two pieces of canvas when a finished seam edge is not required. It is identical to the simple seam used on clothing, but it is sewn ¼ inch from the edge. To make a plain seam—

- Place piece A face up on the sewing table.
- Place piece B face down on top of piece A.
- Adjust the two layers so that the right edges are even.
- Tack the beginning of the seam, and then sew a row of stitches ¼ inch from and parallel to the right edge.
- Tack the end of the seam.

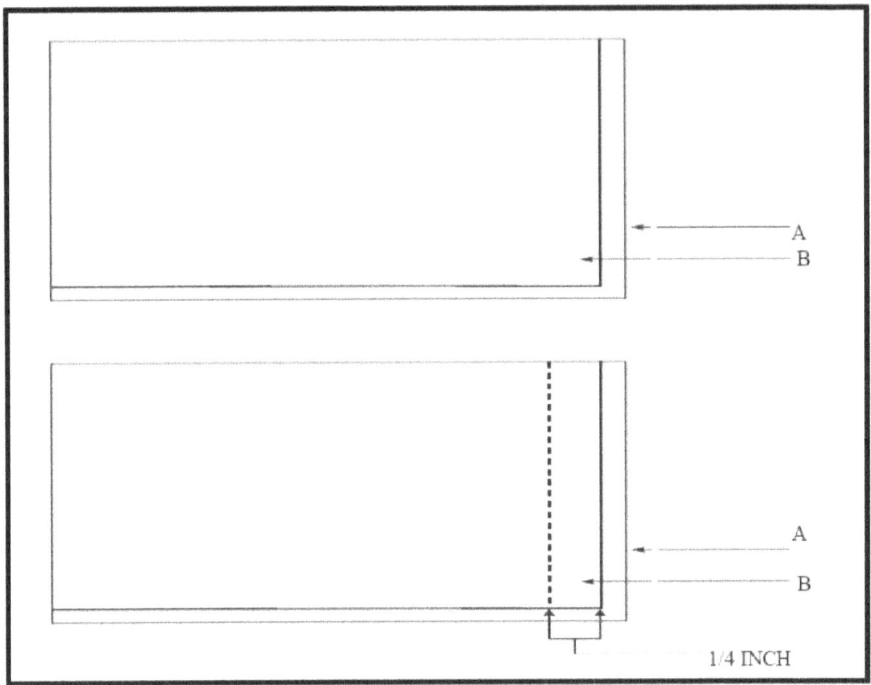

Figure 8-2. Plain seam on canvas

Hemming Seam

8-5. Seam type 1 is a hemming seam. It is similar to the hemming seam used on clothing. The three kinds of hems sewn on canvas are single-edge, grommeted and four-sided—

- Place the piece of canvas face down on a worktable.
- With a ruler and chalk, mark a line 1 inch from the raw edge.
- Fold the raw edge of the canvas up and over to the left until it meets the chalk line to form a ½ inch turn under.
- Crease the folded edges in place with the handle of a pair of shears.
- Mark a second chalk line 2 inches to the left of the folded edge.
- Fold the cloth to the left again until the folded edge meets the second chalk line to form a 1 inch hem.
- Crease the second folded edge in place with the handle of a pair of shears.
- Tack the beginning of the seam, and then sew a row of stitches ⅛ inch to the right of the second folded edge.
- Tack the end of the seam.

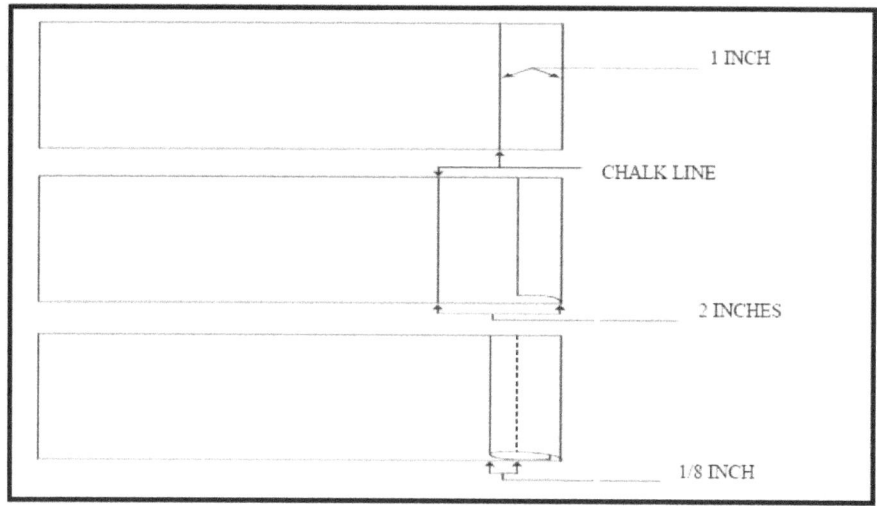

Figure 8-3. Single-edge hem

Grommeted Hem

8-6. A grommeted hem (Figure 8-4) is used to finish an edge where grommets will be installed. Extra fabric is required to give the hem added strength. To sew a grommeted hem—

- Place the piece of canvas face down on a worktable.
- With a ruler and chalk, mark a line 4 inches from the raw edge.
- Fold the raw edge of the canvas up and over to the left until it meets the chalk line to form a 2 inch turn under.
- Crease the folded edge in place with the handle of a pair of shears.
- Mark a second chalk line 4 inches to the left of the folded edge.
- Fold the cloth to the left again until the folded edge meets the second chalk line to form a 2 inch hem.
- Crease the second folded edge in place with the handle of a pair of shears.
- Tack the beginning of the seam, and then sew a row of stitches $\frac{1}{8}$ inch to the right of the second folded edge.
- Tack the end of the seam.

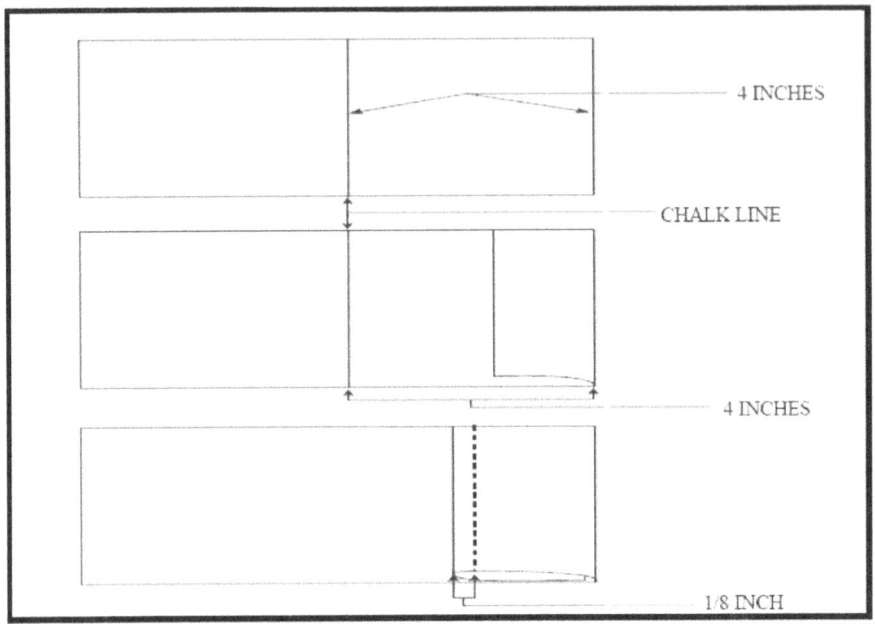

Figure 8-4. Seam type 1—grommeted hem

Four-Sided Hem

8-7. A four-sided hem (Figure 8-5) is used to finish a rectangular piece of canvas completely on all sides. To make a four-sided hem—

- Square a 12 by 12 inch piece of material. Use the straight edge (ruler); make a ½ inch mark on all four sides of the material. After this is completed, use the ruler to connect these marks.

Note: *The ½ inch marks will be your fold lines to be folded under*

- For the hem width using a ruler, mark 1 inch marks from the ½ inch fold line completely around the piece of material. Using a straight edge, align these marks and connect them around the material.

- After completing the above two steps, turn the material over and fold on the ½ inch mark (folding right side, bottom, left side, and then top). Now take the 1 inch mark and do the same.

Note: *Always fold material so that the stitch lines are visible to you. By doing this, you can tell if you are going off, or if the stitch line is crooked.*

- With the folded edge up, place the material under the presser foot and insert the needle ⅛ inch from the inside hem edge. Sew toward the bottom until the needle catches the bottom hem fold ⅛ inch. Turn the material until you have the corner facing you and sew diagonally toward the corner until the needle reaches within ⅛ inch from the corner. Raise the presser foot while the needle is still intact in the material and turn the material so that the stitch line is toward you. Again, turn the material until the stitched hem is at the top. Sew straight down ⅛ inch away from the edge. Sew the remaining corners in the same manner until the needle reaches the starting point. Sew over the stitches previously made 1 inch for tacking.

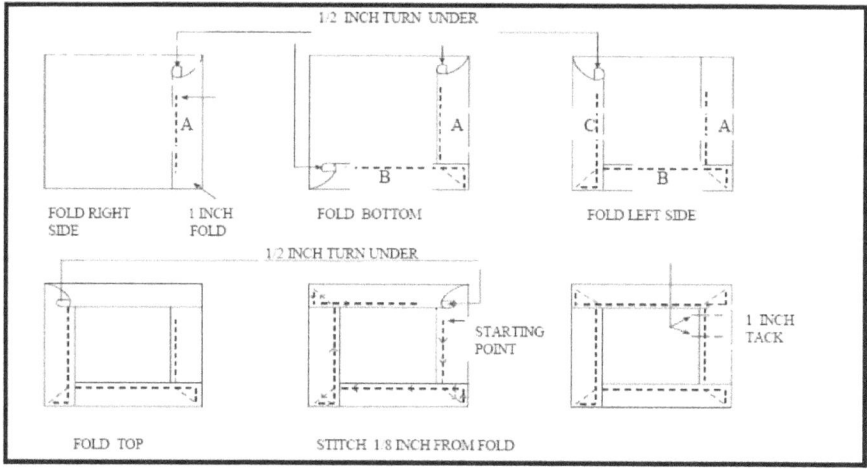

Figure 8-5. Four-sided hem

Flat Seam

8-8. A flat seam (Figure 8-6) is used to join two pieces of canvas that have selvage edges. A selvage edge is a woven edge that will not unravel. A flat seam is used when a seam has to be finished on the outside and the inside, such as the seams of tents, tarpaulins, and truck covers. To make a flat seam—

- Place piece A face up on a worktable with the selvage edge to the left.
- With a ruler and chalk, measure and mark a chalk line 1 inch from and parallel to the selvage edge.
- Place piece B face up on top of piece A so that the selvage edge of B is on the chalk line.
- Tack the beginning of the seam and sew the two pieces together with a row of stitches ⅛ inch to the left of the selvage edge of B. Tack the end of the seam.
- Turn both pieces of canvas face down.
- Tack the beginning of the seam and sew a second row of stitches ⅛ inch to the right of the selvage edge of A. Tack the end of the seam.

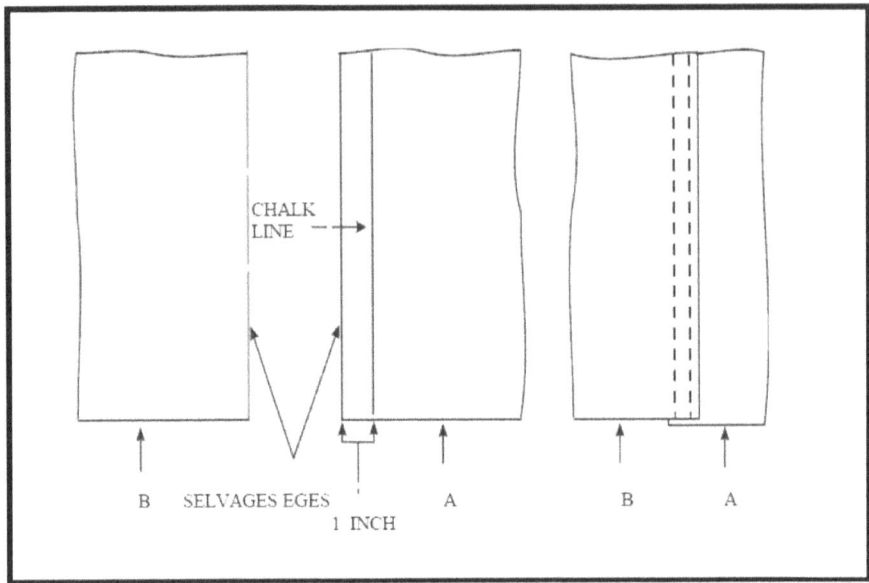

Figure 8-6. Flat seam

Single-Felled Seam

8-9. The single-felled seam (Figure 8-7) is similar to the welt seam used on clothing but the single-felled seam is sewn with two rows of stitches. This seam is used to join two pieces of canvas when the outside has to be finished and the inside does not. It is also used to sew on patches. To make a single-felled seam—

- Sew piece A and B together with a simple seam but stitch the seam 1 inch from the right edge.
- Lift piece A up and over to the right so that both pieces are face up and both seam allowances are to the right underneath.
- Tack the beginning of the seam and sew a row of stitches ⅛ inch to the right of the fold through all three layers (piece A and seam allowances). Tack the end of the seam.
- Turn the pieces face down.
- Tack the beginning of the seam and sew a row of stitches 1//8 inch to the right of the raw edges through all three layers. Tack the end of the seam.

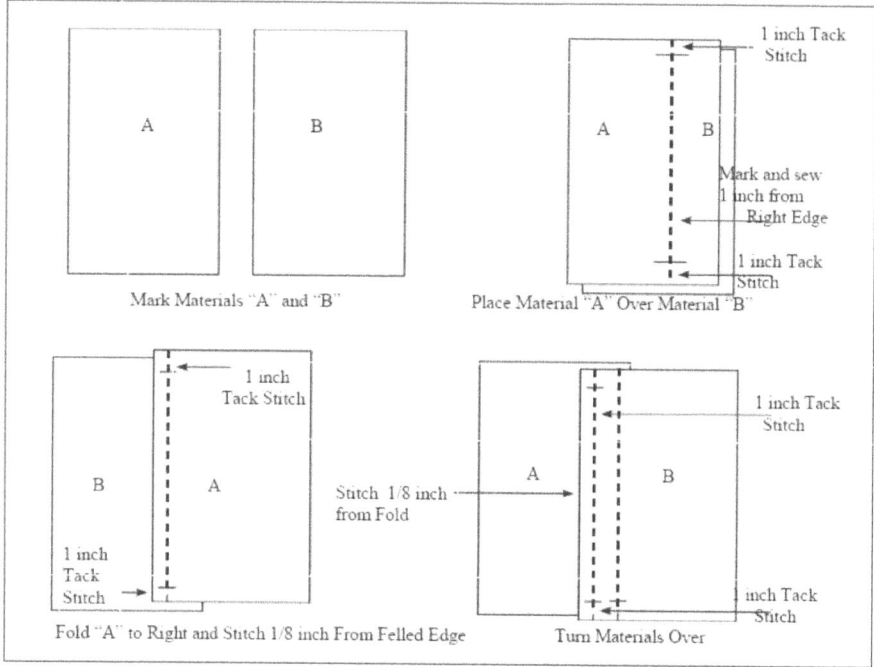

Figure 8-7. Single-felled seam

Double-Felled Seam

8-10. The double-felled seam (Figure 8-8) is similar in appearance to the double-lapped seam used on clothing. This seam is used to join two pieces of canvas when the outside and the inside of the seam have to be finished with no exposed raw edges. To make a double-felled seam—

- Place piece A face up on a worktable.
- With a ruler and chalk, mark a chalk line 1 inch from and parallel to the left edge.
- Place piece B face down on a worktable.
- With a ruler and chalk, mark a chalk line 1 inch from and parallel to the left edge.
- Place piece B face down on piece A. Align the left edge of piece B with the chalk line of piece A.
- Tack the beginning of the seam and sew the two pieces of canvas together by stitching a seam on the chalk line of piece B. Tack the end of the seam.
- Fold the left edge of piece A up and over to the left on the stitch row of B.
- Fold the right side of piece B up and over to the left on the seam line so that both pieces are face up.

93

- Tack the beginning of the seam and sew a row of stitches ⅛ inch to the left of the folded edge. Tack the end of the seam.
- Turn both pieces of canvas over so that they are face down.
- Tack the beginning of the seam and sew another row of stitches ⅛ inch to the left of the folded edge. Tack the end of the seam.

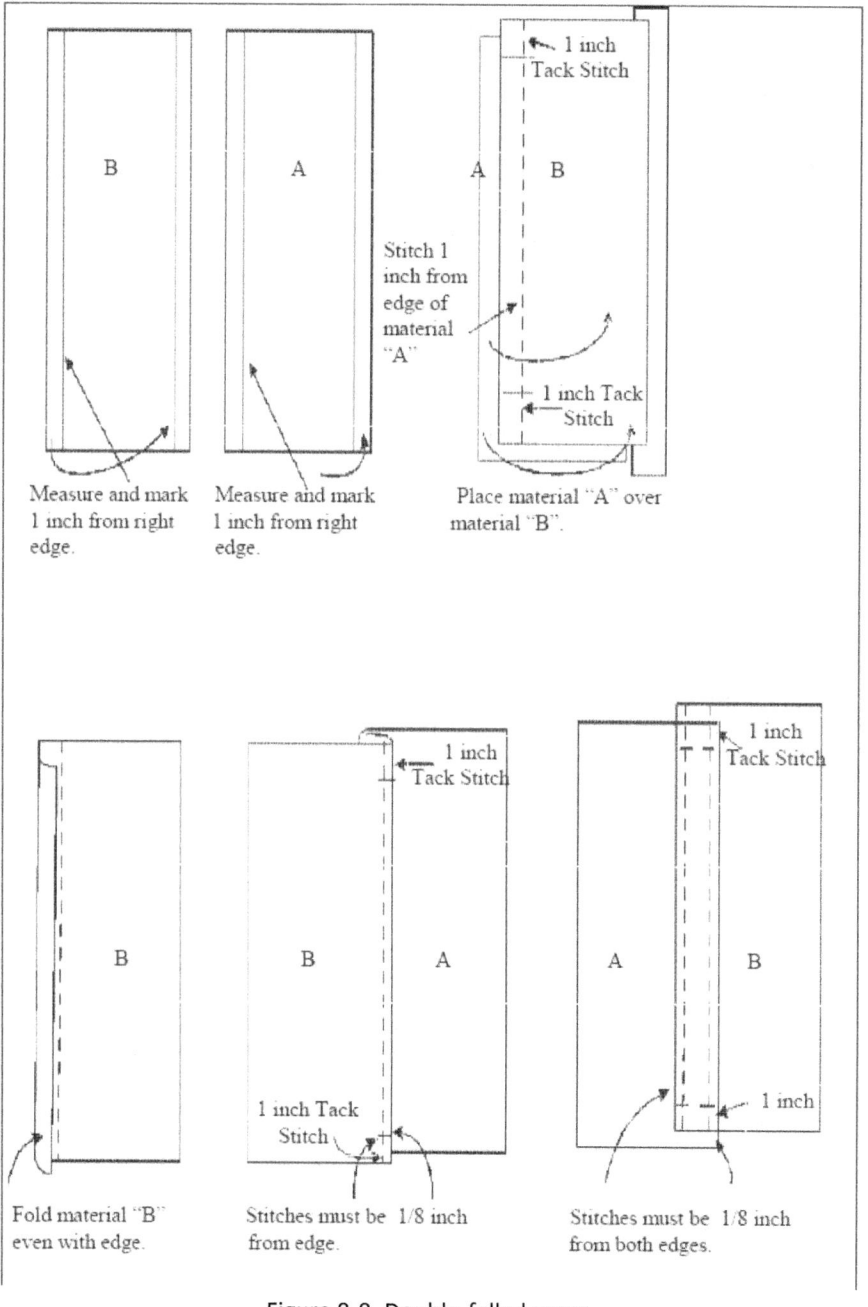

Figure 8-8. Double-felled seam

CHAPTER 9 - SEWING REPAIRS TO CANVAS

SECTION I – Repairing Canvas

9-1. Canvas items are made of duck. Duck is a heavy, closely woven, cotton fabric. It is a sturdy fabric, but like all cotton cloth, it is subject to wear. It weakens with age, washings, and use. Tents and canvas items are mended by fabric repair specialists. Some repairs, such as replacing a rivet, do not require sewing. Repairs which require sewing include darning, patching, remaking buttonholes, and replacing zippers and stovepipe openings.

SECTION II – Darning

9-2. Darns are used to repair small holes and worn areas in all canvas items except tents. Darns are made by machine or by hand. Machine darning is preferred to hand darning. See the appropriate technical manuals for instructions on how to darn on canvas using a darning machine or a heavy-duty sewing machine. The four kinds of darns used on canvas are circular, zigzag, reinforced and overedge.

Circular Darn

9-3. The circular darn is used to repair small holes and worn areas in canvas that measure less than ½ inch across. A circular darn is also used on clothing. The procedures used to make a circular darn are on page 38.

Zigzag Darn

9-4. The zigzag darn is used to repair slits and straight tears in canvas where no fabric is missing. It is used to mend holes in clothing, but not in canvas. The directions for zigzag darn are on page 40.

Reinforced Darn

9-5. The reinforced darn is used to repair holes in canvas that measure ¼ to ¾ inch across. The instructions on page 41-42 describe how to make a reinforced darn.

Overedge Darn

9-6. The overedge darn (Figure 9-1) is used to repair worn corded seams and bindings. It is not used on clothing. To make an overedge darn—
- Turn the canvas item face up.
- Anchor the thread on the underside by sticking the needle up through the canvas near the cording.
- Stick the needle back down into the canvas on the other side of the cording.

- Continue to stitch around the cording in a circular or overhand fashion until the damaged area is covered.
- Knot the thread on the underside near the cording and cut the thread close to the knot.

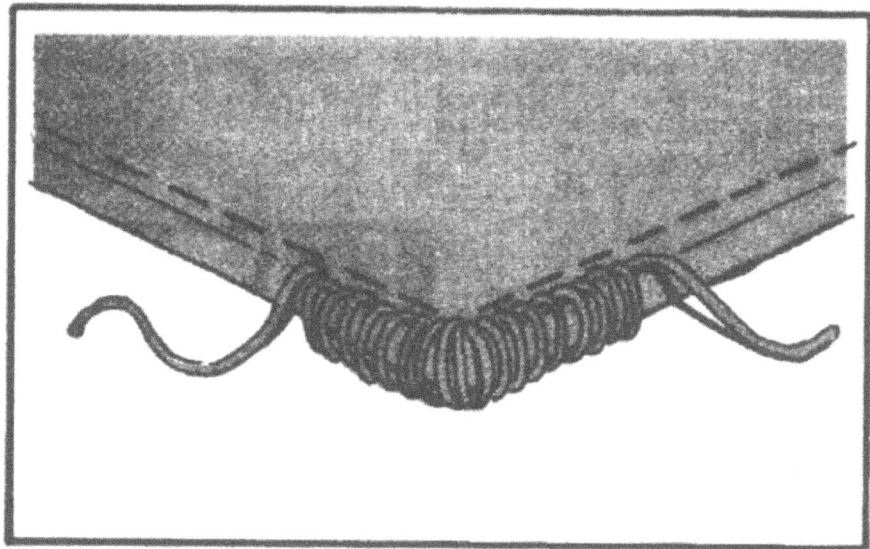

Figure 9-1. Overedge darn

SECTION III – Patching

9-7. Patches are used to repair holes and tears in tents. They are used to repair holes and tears that measure more than ¾ inch across in other canvas items. Patches are used also to repair large worn areas of canvas. Patches are cut from scrapped canvas which is the same color and texture as the canvas to be mended. Items made of waterproof, fire-resistant, and mildew-resistant canvas are patched with canvas that has received the same protective treatment. Several kinds of patches are used to repair canvas. They are described below.

Simple Canvas Patch

9-8. The simple canvas patch is sewn over or under the damaged area of canvas. The two kinds of simple canvas patches are the top patch and the inverted patch.

Simple Canvas Top Patch

9-9. A simple canvas top patch (Figure 9-2) is sewn to the top side of canvas. It is the easiest patch to make and to attach to damaged canvas. To make the simple canvas top patch-

Zigzag darn the edges of a rip or tear together to prevent further damage, if no canvas is missing. If canvas is missing, cut out the damaged area in the shape of a rectangle.

97

- Place the damaged area face up on a worktable.
- Measure the damaged area.
- Cut a rectangular patch from matching canvas. Make the patch large enough to extend 2 ¾ inches beyond the damaged are on all four sides.
- Place the patch face up on a worktable.
- Draw chalk lines ¾ inch from all four raw edges.
- Fold under the raw edges on the chalk lines and crease the folded edges in place with the handle of a pair of shears.
- Center the patch face up on top of the damaged area.
- Sew on the patch by stitching a seam ⅛ inch from the folded edges on all four sides of the patch. Pivot the canvas and patch on the needle at the corners.
- Sew over the first stitches for at least 1 inch to tack the seam.

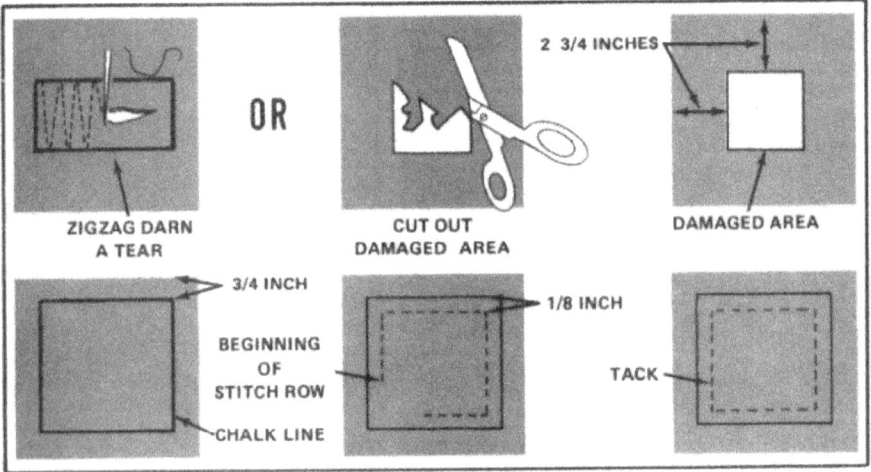

Figure 9-2. Simple canvas top patch

Simple Canvas Inverted Patch

9-10. A simple canvas inverted patch (Figure 9-3) is sewn to the inside or the underside of the canvas. To make this patch, follow the directions in the previous paragraph, but center the patch on the underside of the canvas and secure it in place.

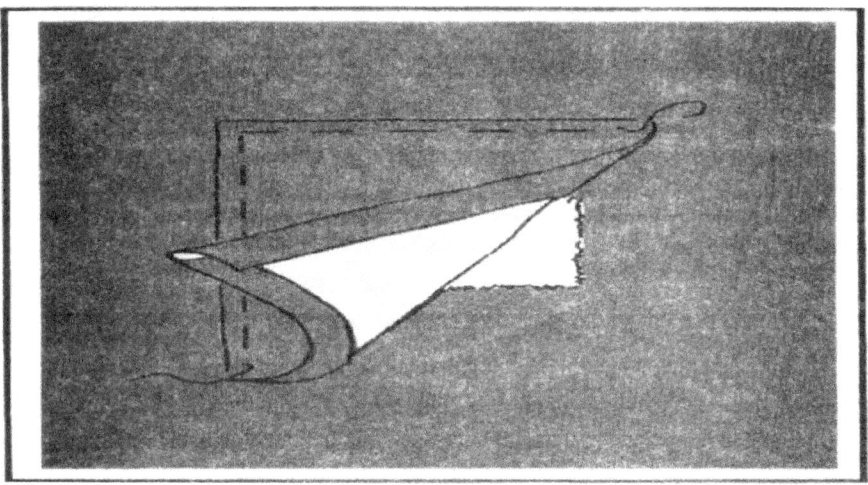

Figure 9-3. Simple canvas inverted patch

Felled Canvas Patch

9-11. The felled canvas patch, like the simple canvas patch, is sewn over or under a damaged area of canvas. Unlike the simple canvas patch, the raw edges of the damaged area are trimmed and neatly finished. The two kinds of felled canvas patches are the top patch and the inverted patch.

Felled Canvas Top Patch

9-12. The felled canvas top patch (Figure 9-4) is sewn to the top side of canvas. To make a felled canvas top patch--

- Cut out the damaged area in the shape of a rectangle.
- Place the damaged area face up on a worktable.
- Measure the damaged area.
- Cut a rectangular patch from matching canvas. Make the patch large enough to extend 2 ¾ inches beyond the damaged area on all four sides.
- Place the patch face up on a worktable.
- Draw chalk lines ¾ inch from all four raw edges.
- Fold under the raw edges on the chalk lines and crease the folded edges in place.
- Center the patch face up on top of the damaged area.
- Sew on the patch by stitching a seam ⅛ inch from the folded edges on all four sides of the patch. Pivot the canvas and patch on the needle at each corner. Sew over the first stitches for at least 1 inch to tack the seam.
- On the underside, measure ½ inch from each side of the cutout area and draw a rectangle with chalk.
- Clip each corner of the cutout area diagonally.

- Fold under the raw edges ½ inch and crease the folded edges in place with the handle of a pair of shears.
- Stitch a seam around the hole ⅛ inch from the folded edges. Sew over the first stitches for at least 1 inch to tack the seam.

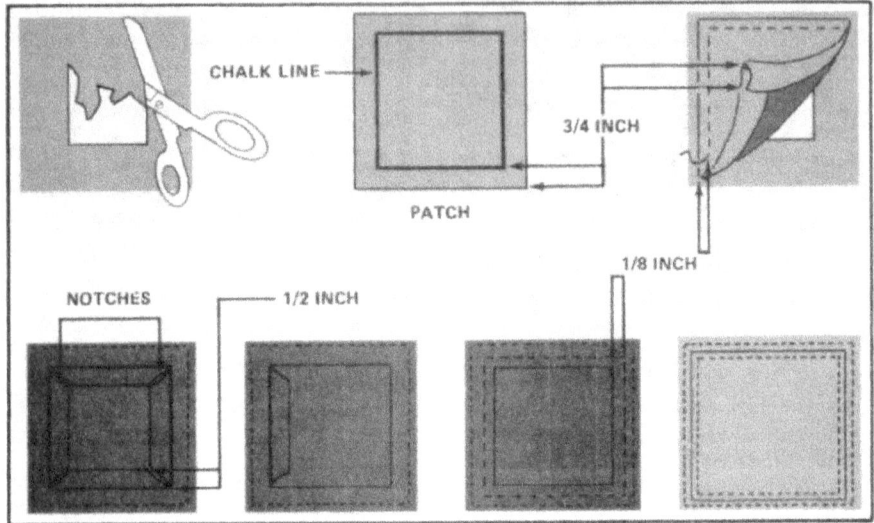

Figure 9-4. Felled canvas top patch

Felled Canvas Inverted Patch

9-13. A felled canvas inverted patch (Figure 9-5) is sewn to the inside or the underside of canvas. To make this patch, follow the directions given in the previous paragraph, but center the patch face up on the damaged area on the underside of the canvas and secure it in place. Clip the corners on the topside of the canvas, fold the tabs under, and stitch them in place.

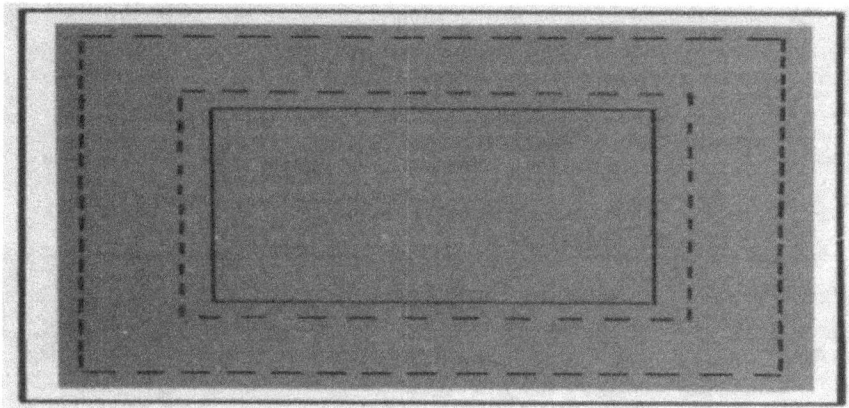

Figure 9-5. Felled canvas inverted patch

Watershed Patch

9-14. The watershed patch (Figure 9-6) is a five-sided patch used on the outside of tents. The slant of the two top edges allows water to run off so that it does not collect in the top edge seaming. For this reason, the watershed patch lasts longer than a rectangular patch. Using a watershed patch to repair a tent is preferable to using a rectangular patch. However, a rectangular patch can be used under an eave where the top edge is protected. It can also be used to straddle a ridge on a tent where the top and bottom of the patch are slanted toward the ground. To make a watershed patch—

- Measure the damaged area.
- Cut a patch from matching canvas. Make the patch large enough to extend 2 ¾ inches beyond the damaged area on all four sides.
- Fold the patch in half lengthwise. Crease the folded edge with the handle of a pair of shears.
- Unfold the patch.
- Fold the top right-hand corner to the crease in the center.
- Fold the top left hand corner even with the right-hand corner and crease these folds in place.
- Fold the inside corner of each triangle to the edge of the outside fold. Crease these folds in place.
- Unfold the patch. Cut off the top corners, using the creases closest to the corners as cutting lines.
- Turn the patch face up.
- Draw chalk lines ¾ inch from the raw edges.
- Fold under the raw edges on the chalk lines and crease the folded edges in place.
- Center the patch on the damaged area so that the slanted edges at the top of the patch will point upward on an erect tent.

- Sew the patch to the tent by stitching a seam ⅛ inch from the folded edges. Pivot the canvas and the patch on the needle at the corners. Tack the seam by stitching over the first stitches for at least 1 inch.
- Sew a second seam ⅜ to ½ inch inside the first seam. Tack the seam for at least 1 inch.
- Cut out the damaged area on the inside of the tent to within ⅛ inch of the second seam.

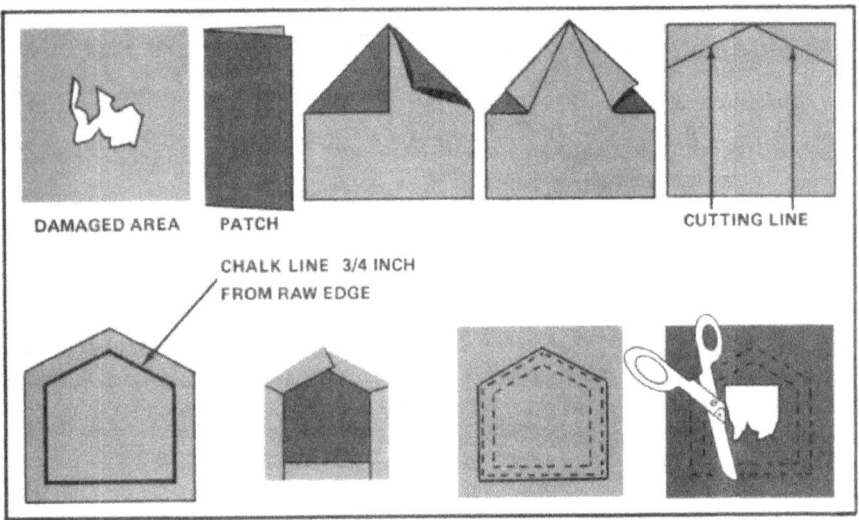

Figure 9-6. Watershed patch

Seam Patch

9-15. A seam patch is a patch sewn over or next to a seam in a canvas item. The seam patch can be rectangular or slanted at the top so that it sheds water better. There are several kinds of seam patches. They are described below.

Under-Seam Patch

9-16. An under-seam patch (Figure 9-7) is used to repair damage near a seam in a canvas item. An underseam patch can be rectangular if it is used on a canvas item other than a tent. It can also be rectangular if it is sewn under an eave or on the ridge of a tent. All other under-seam patches on tents should be slanted at the top to shed water. To make an under-seam patch--

- Open the seam next to the damaged area by cutting through one row of stitches 6 inches above and below the damaged area.
- Measure the damaged area.
- Cut a rectangular patch large enough to extend inside the open seam on one side and 2 ¾ inches beyond the damage on the other three sides.

- Determine which top corner will not be tucked into the seam if the patch should be slanted to shed water. Fold that corner down until it aligns with the side that will be tucked in the seam. Crease the folded edge in place. Fold the corner back to the crease. Crease the second folded edge in place. Unfold the patch. Cut off the top corner, using the top crease as a cutting line.
- Place the patch face up on a worktable.
- Draw chalk lines ¾ inch from the raw edges on three sides. Do not mark on the side that will be tucked into the seam.
- Turn under the three edges on the chalk lines and crease the folded edges in place.
- Center the patch face up over the damage. Position a watershed patch so that the slanted side will be at the top on an erect tent.
- Tuck the flat raw edge of the patch into the open seam.
- Sew the patch to the tent or canvas item by stitching ⅛ inch from the folded edges on three sides. Tack the seam for at least 1 inch.
- Sew the fourth side in place. Close the open seam by stitching a seam 1 inch above the opening to 1 inch below the opening. Tack the seam at each end for at least 1 inch. Use the previous seam line as a stitching guide.
- Sew a second seam ⅜ to ½ inch inside the first seam. Tack the seam at each end for at least 1 inch.
- Cut out the damaged area on the underside to within ⅛ inch of the second seam.

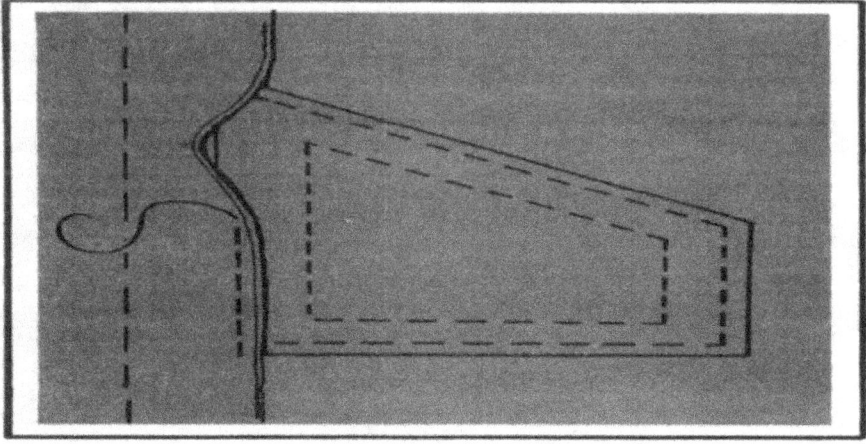

Figure 9-7. Under-seam patch

On-Seam Patch

9-17. An on-seam patch (Figure 9-8) is like an under-seam patch in that it is used to repair damage near a seam in a canvas item. It differs from the under-seam patch in that it overlaps the seam. To make an on-seam patch--

103

- Open the seam next to the damaged area by cutting through on row of stitches 6 inches above and below the damage.
- Measure the damaged area.
- Cut a rectangular patch from matching canvas. Make the patch large enough to overlap the seam on one side and extend 2 ¾ inches beyond the damage on the other three sides.
- Determine which corner will not overlap the seam if the patch should be slanted to shed water. Turn that corner down until it aligns with the side that will overlap the seam. Crease the folded edge in place. Fold the corner back to the crease. Crease the second folded edge in place. Unfold the patch. Cut off the top corner, using the top crease as a cutting line.
- Place the patch face up on a worktable.
- Draw chalk lines ¾ inch from the raw edges on three sides. Do not mark on the side that will overlap the seam.
- Turn under the edges on the chalk line and crease the folded edges in place.
- Turn the patch face down.
- Tuck the flat raw edge of the patch into the open seam.
- Hold the flat raw edge in place so that the patch does not slip out of the open seam. Fold the patch up and over to the opposite side so that the patch is now face up and centered over the damage.
- Sew a seam ⅛ inch from the folded edge on the three sides that are not overlapping the seam. Tack the seam at each end for at least 1 inch.
- Sew a second seam ⅜ to ½ inch inside the first seam. Tack the seam at each end for at least 1 inch.
- Sew the fourth side in place. Close the open seam by stitching a seam 1 inch above the opening to 1 inch below the opening. Use the previous seam line as a stitching guide.
- Sew a second seam inside the seam just sewn. Use the previous seam line as a stitching line. Match stitch rows exactly.
- Cut out the damaged area on the underside to within ⅛ inch of the inside seam.

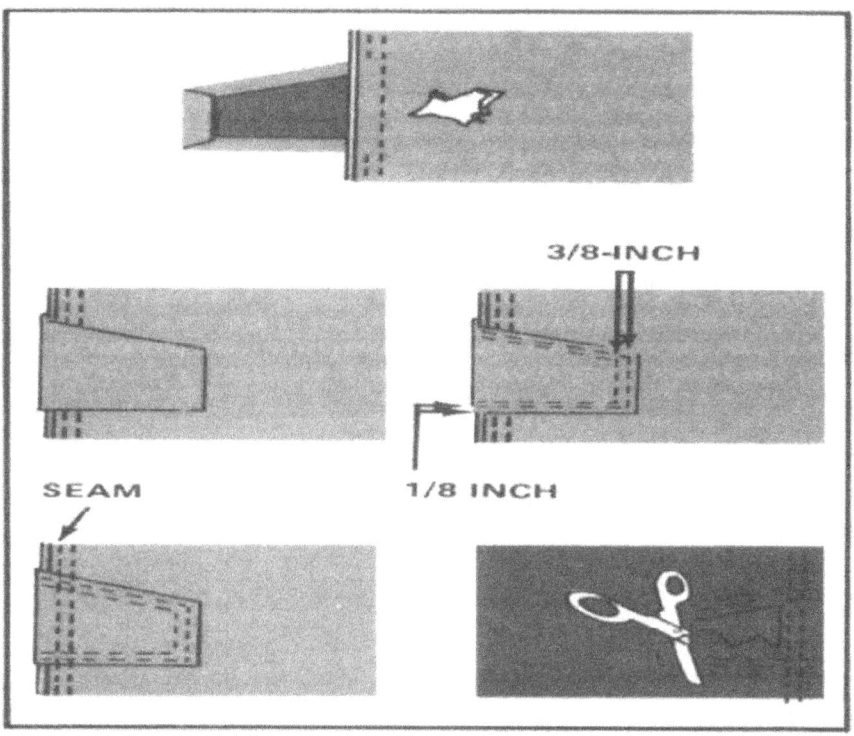

Figure 9-8. On-seam patch

Over-Seam Watershed Patch

9-18. An over-seam watershed patch (Figure 9-9) is a combination of the slanted under-seam and on-seam patches. It is used on tents when there is damage at a seam. To make an over-seam watershed patch--

- Open the seam by cutting through the stitches in both seam lines from 6 inches above the damage to 6 inches below the damage.
- Measure the damaged area.
- Cut a rectangular patch from matching canvas. Make the patch large enough to extend 2 ¾ inches beyond the damage on all sides. Consider the seam overlap and add one seam width for a flat seam, two seam widths for a single-felled seam and three seam widths for a double-felled seam.
- Fold the patch in half lengthwise. Crease the folded edge in place.
- Unfold the patch and fold the two top corners to the crease in the center. Crease the folded edges in place.
- Fold the corners back to the creases. Crease the second folded edges in place.
- Unfold the patch. Cut off the top corners, using the creases closest to the corners as cutting lines.

- Turn the patch face up. Draw chalk lines ¾ inch from the raw edges.
- Fold the raw edges under on the chalk lines and crease the folded edges in place.
- Cut the patch in half, using the crease line in the center as a cutting line.
- Place one of the pieces face up on the damaged area so that the patch will point upward on an erect tent.
- Tuck the flat raw edge of the piece into the open seam. Sew this piece to the tent by stitching ⅛ inch from the folded edges on three sides. Sew a second seam ⅜ to ½ inch inside the first seam. Tack all seams at each end for at least 1 inch.
- Place the other piece face down on top of the first piece. Tuck the flat raw edge into the seam opening.
- Hold the flat raw edge in place so that the piece does not slip out of the open seam. Fold the piece up and over to the opposite side so that it is face up.
- Sew this piece to the tent by stitching ⅛ inch from the folded edges on the three sides. Sew a second seam ⅜ to ⅛ inch inside the first seam. Tack all seams at each end for at least 1 inch.
- Close the open seam by sewing two seams from 1 inch above the opening to 1 inch below the opening. Use the original seam lines as stitching guides. Tack the seams at each end.

Note: On a double-felled seam, turn the canvas to the opposite side and tuck the raw edge under before sewing the second seam.

- Cut out the damaged area on the underside to within ⅛ inch of the inside seam.

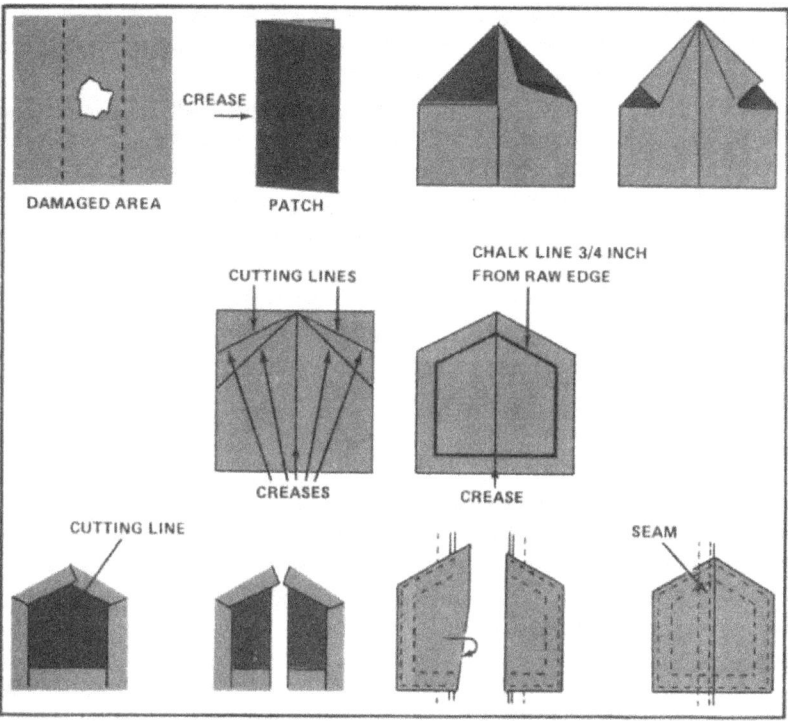

Figure 9-9. Over-seam watershed patch

Seam-to-Seam Patch

9-19. A seam-to-seam patch (Figure 9-10) is used to repair damage between two seams. It is sewn in place so that the canvas and patch overlap like the shingles on a roof. This allows water to run off the top and bottom seams of the patch. To make a seam-to-seam patch on a canvas item with double-felled seams—

- Measure and mark chalk lines from seam to seam 2 inches above and 2 inches below the damage. These chalk lines are cutting lines.
- Measure and mark two chalk lines ½ inch and 1 ½ inches above the top cutting line. Measure and mark two chalk lines ½ and 1 ½ inches below the bottom cutting line. These chalk lines are guidelines.
- Open the seams on each side of the damage by cutting through the stitches from the top guideline to the bottom guideline.
- Cut out the damaged area on the cutting lines.
- Measure the cutout area. Cut a patch from matching canvas 3 inches longer and 3 inches wider than the cutout area. (The extra canvas is used in a 1 inch seam overlap and a ½ inch turn under on each of the four sides.)
- Turn the patch face up. Measure and mark chalk lines ½ inch from the raw edges on all four sides.

107

- Fold under the raw edge of the patch on the chalk line on the bottom and the raw edge on the side that will overlap the canvas item. Crease the folded edges in place.
- Fold up the raw edge of the patch on the chalk line on the top and the raw edge on the side that will be tucked under the canvas item. Crease the folded edge in place.
- Fold under the raw edge of the canvas item $\frac{1}{2}$ inch at the top of the cutout area. Crease the folded edges in place.
- Fold up the raw edges of the canvas item $\frac{1}{2}$ inch at the bottom of the cutout area. Crease the folded edge in place.
- Tuck the top edge of the patch under the top edge of the cutout area. Overlap the patch by 1 inch, using the top chalk line on the canvas item as a guide.
- Center the patch from side to side. Tuck under or overlap the sides of the patch by 1 inch.
- Stitch the top edge in place by sewing a seam $\frac{1}{8}$ inch from the folded edge of the cutout area.
- Sew a second seam $\frac{3}{8}$ to $\frac{1}{2}$ inch above the first seam.
- Overlap the bottom edge of the cutout area 1 inch with the bottom edge of the patch.
- Stitch the bottom edge in place by sewing a seam $\frac{1}{8}$ inch from the folded edge of the patch.
- Sew a second seam $\frac{3}{8}$ to $\frac{1}{2}$ inch above the first seam.
- Stitch each side in place, using the original seam lines as stitching guides. Tack each seam for at least 1 inch

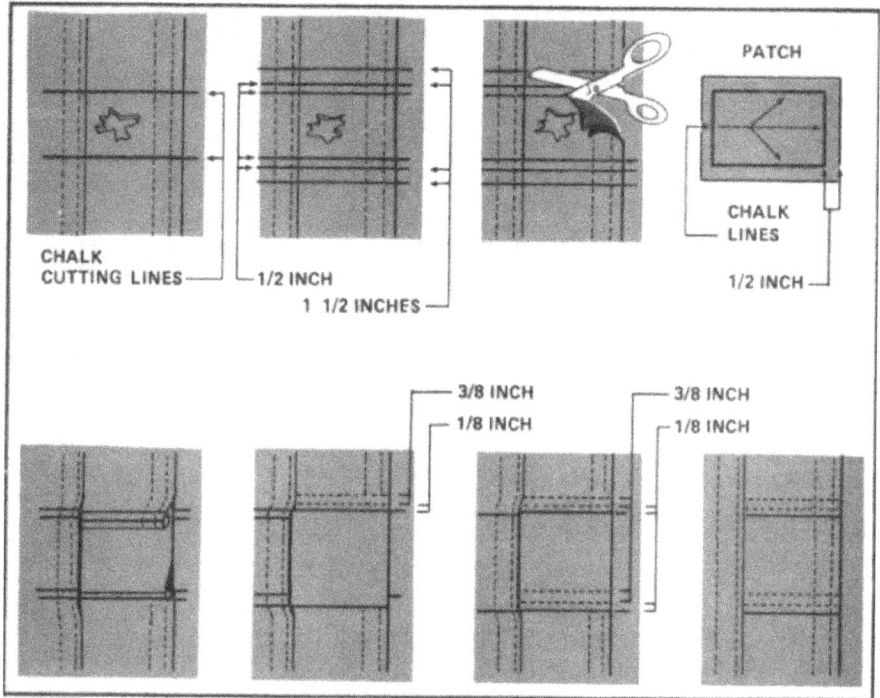

Figure 9-10. Seam-to-seam patch

Eave-Edge Patch

9-20. An eave-edge patch (Figure 9-11) is used to repair damage on the eave of a tent. It is sewn to both sides of the eave. To make an eave-edge patch—

- Measure the width of the eave.
- Measure the length of the damaged area.
- Cut a patch from matching canvas. Make it four times as wide as the eave. Make it long enough to extend 2 ½ inches beyond the damage on the left and right sides.
- Turn the patch face up. Draw chalk lines ½ inch from the left and right sides.
- Fold under the left and right raw edges along the chalk lines. Crease the folded edges in place.
- Turn the patch face down. Measure and mark a horizontal chalk line in the center of the patch.
- Draw chalk lines ⅛ inch above and below the center chalk line.
- Fold the patch in half on the center chalk line. Crease the folded edge in place.
- Fold the top and bottom raw edges toward the center until the edges meet the ⅛ inch chalk lines. Crease the folded edges in place.

109

- Wrap the patch around the eave so that the fold in the center of the patch is on the bottom edge of the eave. Center the patch over the damage.
- Stitch the patch in place by sewing a seam ⅛ inch from the folded edges on the top half of the patch. Stitch through all layers. Tack the seam for at least 1 inch by sewing over the first stitches.

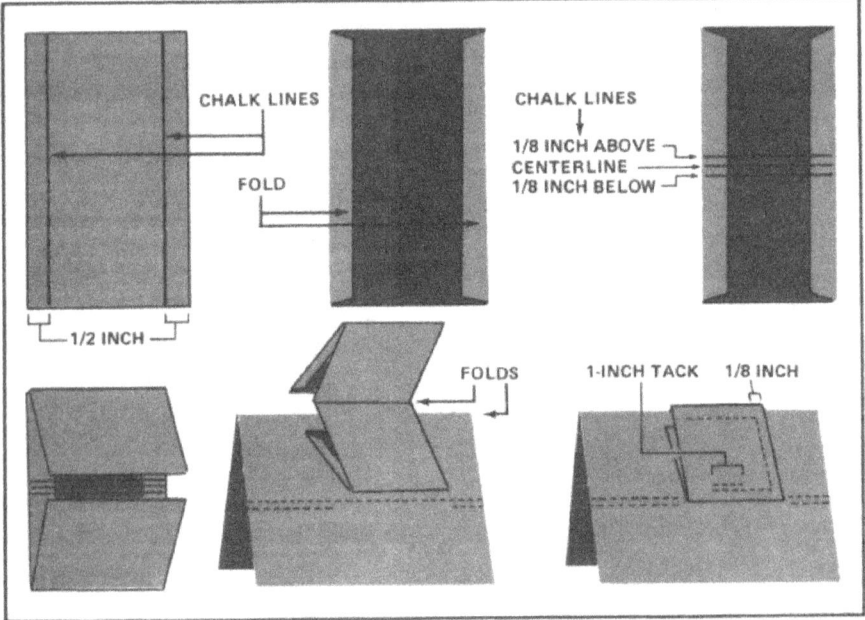

Figure 9-11. Eave-edge patch

Tarpaulin Patch

9-21. A tarpaulin patch (Figure 9-12) is used to repair protective canvas corners. The patch is triangular so that it can shed water easily when the tarpaulin is draped over objects. To make a tarpaulin patch—

- Measure the damage.
- Cut a three-sided patch from matching canvas. Make the patch large enough to extend 2 ¾ to 3 ¾ inches beyond the damage on all three sides.
- Turn the patch face up. Draw chalk lines ¾ inch from the raw edges on all three sides.
- Turn under the raw edges on the chalk lines and crease the folded edges in place. (If the damage is near a seam, tuck one side of the patch into the seam.)
- Stitch the patch in place by sewing a seam around the three sides ⅛ inch from the folded edges. Tack the seam for at least 1 inch.

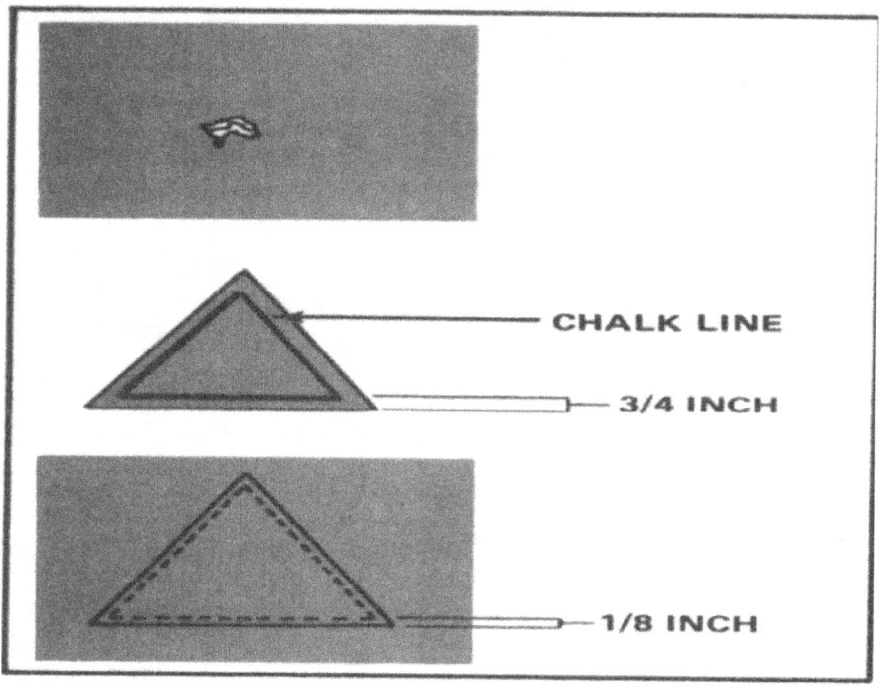

Figure 9-12. Tarpaulin patch

STRAP-SUPPORT PATCH

9-22. A strap-support patch is used to repair a damaged area where a strap was attached. The patch is made from salvaged canvas with a strap attached. The two kinds of strap-support patches are single-thickness and double-thickness.

Single-Thickness

9-23. The single-thickness patch (Figure 9-13) is made of one layer of canvas. It is used when the strain on the strap is slight and there is little chance of the patch being pulled loose. To make a single-thickness patch--

- Cut out the damaged area.
- Measure the cutout area.
- Cut a patch from salvaged canvas with a strap attached. Make the patch large enough to extend 2 ¾ inches beyond the cutout area on all sides.
- Turn the patch face up. Measure and mark a chalk line ¾ inch from the raw edges on all sides.
- Turn up the raw edges along the chalk lines, and crease the folded edges in place.
- Turn the canvas item face down.
- Draw chalk lines ½ inch from the raw edges on all sides of the cutout area.
- Notch each corner to the chalk line.

111

- Turn up the raw edges along the chalk line and crease the folded edges in place.
- Turn the canvas item face up.
- Center the patch face up under the cutout area.
- Stitch a seam around the cutout area ⅛ inch from the folded edges on all sides. Tack the seam for at least 1 inch.
- Turn the canvas item face down. Stitch a seam around the patch ⅛ inch from the folded edges on all sides. Tack the seam for at least 1 inch.

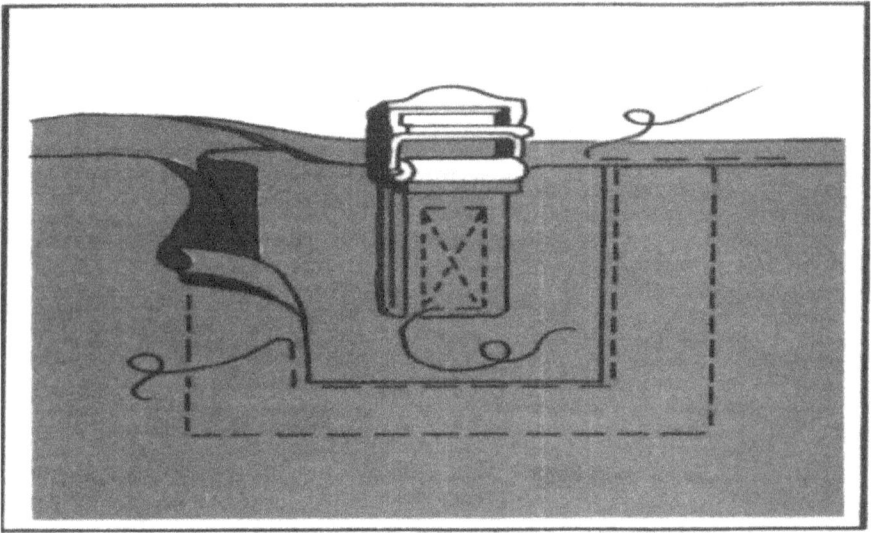

Figure 9-13. Single-thickness patch

Double-Thickness

9-24. A double-thickness patch (Figure 9-14) consists of a top patch and an inverted patch. It is used when a strap gets a lot of strain and an extra layer of canvas is needed to give strength to the repair. To make a double-thickness patch--

- Measure the damage.
- Cut a top patch with a strap attached and an inverted patch from salvaged matching canvas. Make the patches large enough to extend 2 ¾ inches beyond the damage on all sides.
- Turn the patches face up. Draw chalk lines ¾ inch from all raw edges on both patches.
- Turn under all raw edges on the patches along the chalk lines. Crease the folded edges in place.
- Turn the damaged canvas item over and center the inverted patch over the damage.
- Sew the inverted patch in place by stitching a seam ⅛ inch from the folded edges on all sides. Tack the seam for at least 1 inch.

112

- Turn the canvas item face up and cut out the damaged area to within ⅛ inch of the stitch line.
- Center the top patch on top of the cutout area. Align the top patch with the inverted patch.
- Sew the top patch in place by stitching a seam ⅛ inch from the folded edges on all sides. Tack the seam for at least 1 inch.

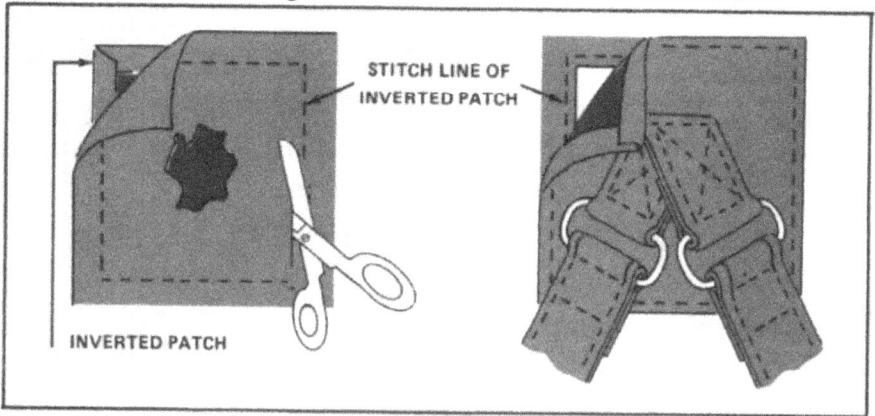

STITCH LINE OF INVERTED PATCH

INVERTED PATCH

Figure 9-14. Double-thickness patch

Grommet Patch

9-25. A grommet patch is used to repair the canvas where a grommet has been torn loose. The two kinds of grommet patches are overedge and reinforced.

Overedge Grommet Patch

9-26. An overedge grommet patch (Figure 9-15) is used to repair the damage when a grommet near an edge has been torn loose. There are two ways to make the repair. If the grommet was located on an eave or bottom edge, use an eave-edge patch to repair the damage. After the canvas has been repaired, insert a grommet. If the grommet was located in an area other than an eave or a bottom edge--

- Measure the damaged area.
- Cut a patch from matching canvas. Make it large enough to fold over and cover the damage on the top side and the underside. Make it large enough to extend 2 ¾ inches beyond the damage on all sides.
- Turn the patch face up.
- Draw chalk lines ¾ inch from the raw edges on all sides.
- Fold under the raw edges along the chalk lines. Crease the folded edges in place.
- Fold the patch in half and lap it over the edge of the damaged canvas.

113

- Sew the patch in place by stitching a seam around the patch ⅛ inch from the folded edges. Sew through all layers. Tack the seam for at least 1 inch.
- Insert a grommet. (If canvas with a row of grommets was damaged, replace the entire section with one patch and a row of new grommets.)

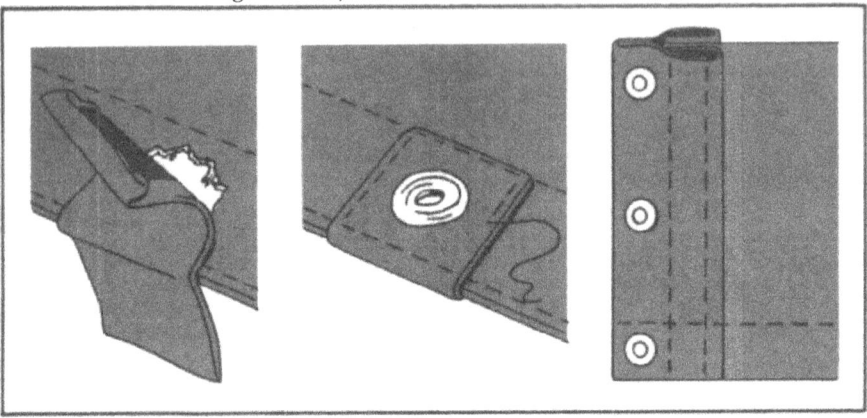

Figure 9-15. Overedge grommet patches

Reinforce Grommet Patch

9-27. A reinforced grommet patch (Figure 9-16) is used to repair the damage when a grommet near a corner has been torn loose. The patch consists of two patches and canvas reinforcement. The three layers of canvas give strength to the repair. To make a reinforced grommet patch--

- Cut out the damaged corner.
- Measure the length and width of the cutout area.
- Cut one piece of canvas for reinforcement the same size as the cutout area. Set it aside.
- Cut two patches from matching canvas but make them 4 inches wider and 2 inches longer than the cutout area.
- Turn the patches face up. Measure and mark chalk lines ½ inch from all raw edges on both patches.
- Fold under all raw edges along the chalk lines on both patches. Crease the folded edges in place.
- Turn the canvas item face down. Place one patch face up on top of the missing corner. Align the edges exactly.
- Sew the patch to the canvas item by stitching ⅛ inch from the folded edges on two sides of the patch.
- Turn the canvas item face up. Set the piece of canvas reinforcement in the cutout area on top of the patched corner. Align the edges with the folded edges of the patch.

- Place the other patch face up on top of the reinforcement piece of canvas. Align all folded edges of the patches.
- Sew the patch in place by stitching a seam ⅛ inch from the folded edges on all four sides. Tack the seam for at least 1 inch.
- Insert a grommet.

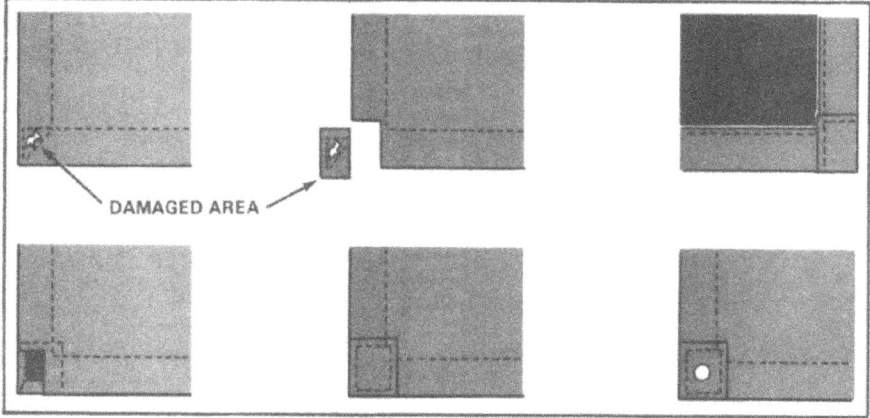

Figure 9-16. Reinforced grommet patch

SECTION IV – Replacing Stovepipe Openings

9-28. A stovepipe opening is an outlet on the roof of a tent. The opening can be damaged a great deal by sparks and heat. Instead of scrapping the entire tent, replace the damaged opening with an opening salvaged from another tent. If no salvaged opening is available, fabric repair specialists can make a new one out of canvas. To replace a stovepipe opening (Figure 9-17)—

- Draw chalk lines from seam to seam 2 inches above and below the stovepipe stitching.
- Open the panel seams on each of the stovepipe opening.
- Cut out the damaged stovepipe opening along the chalk lines.
- Cut a replacement panel from a piece of matching canvas. Make it large enough to extend 1 ½ inches beyond the edges of the cutout area on all four sides.
- Measure the width and length of the reinforcement piece on the damaged opening. Cut a replacement piece from matching canvas. Make the piece 1 inch wider and 2 inches longer than the reinforcement piece.
- Turn the reinforcement piece face up. Mark an outline of the stovepipe opening on the reinforcement piece. Draw it the same size and in the same place as the original stovepipe opening.
- Turn the replacement panel face up. Center the reinforcement piece face up on top of the replacement panel.
- Sew the two pieces together by stitching a seam around the outline of the stovepipe opening.

115

- Make an opening for the stovepipe by cutting a hole through both pieces within ⅛ inch of the chalk line.
- Tuck all four corners of the reinforcement piece into the hole and pull the canvas through to the other side.
- Turn both pieces so that they are face down. Flatten out the two pieces and stitch around the opening ⅛ inch from the edge. Tack the seam at least 1 inch.
- Fold under the raw edges of the reinforcement piece ½ inch on all four sides.
- Stitch around the reinforcement piece by sewing a seam ⅛ inch from the folded edges. Tack the seam at least 1 inch.
- Turn the two pieces face up.
- Make replacement flaps with ties. Make the same type and size as the flaps on the original stovepipe opening.
- Stitch the right flap in place.
- Stitch the left flap in place.
- Stitch the top flap in place.
- Sew the new opening to the tent. Stitch it in place the same way a seam-to-seam patch is sewn in place.

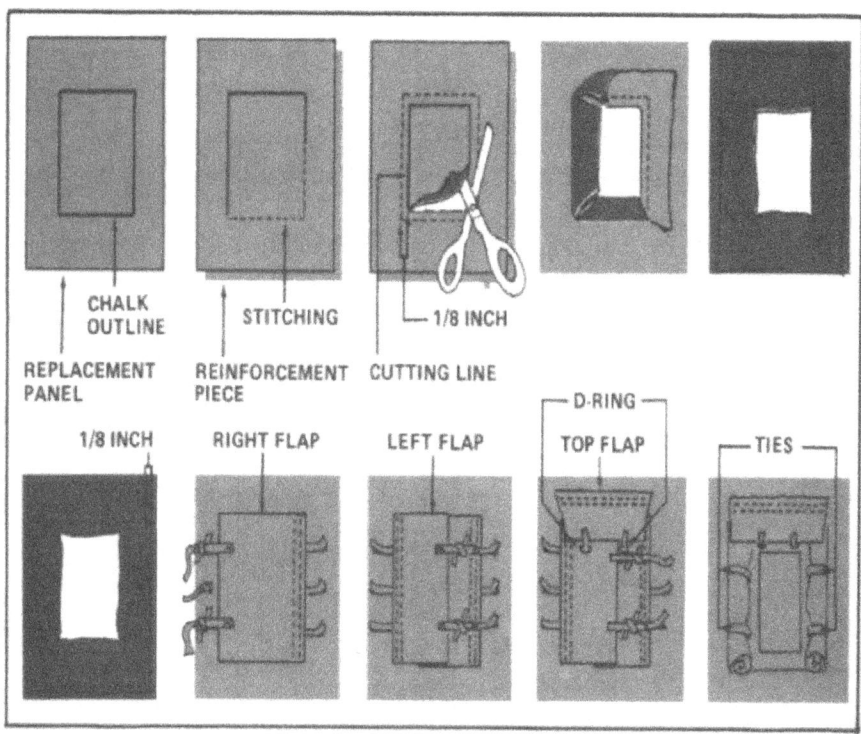

Figure 9-17. Replacing a stovepipe opening

SECTION V – Remaking Buttonholes

9-29. Buttonholes and tack buttons are used on canvas items and tents to close openings. The thread around the buttonholes can unravel and the surrounding canvas can tear. The fabric repair specialist remakes damaged buttonholes using one of three methods.

Felled Patch Method

9-30. To make a buttonhole using the felled patch method (Figure 9-18)—

- Cut a patch from matching canvas. If possible, use a salvaged piece of canvas that has a buttonhole in it.
- Follow the directions on page 99 to apply a felled canvas top patch, but finish the edge of the opening with a binding.
- If the patch does not have a buttonhole, make one by cutting a slit as long as the original buttonhole. Reinforce the raw edges by stitching around the slit using the buttonhole stitch.

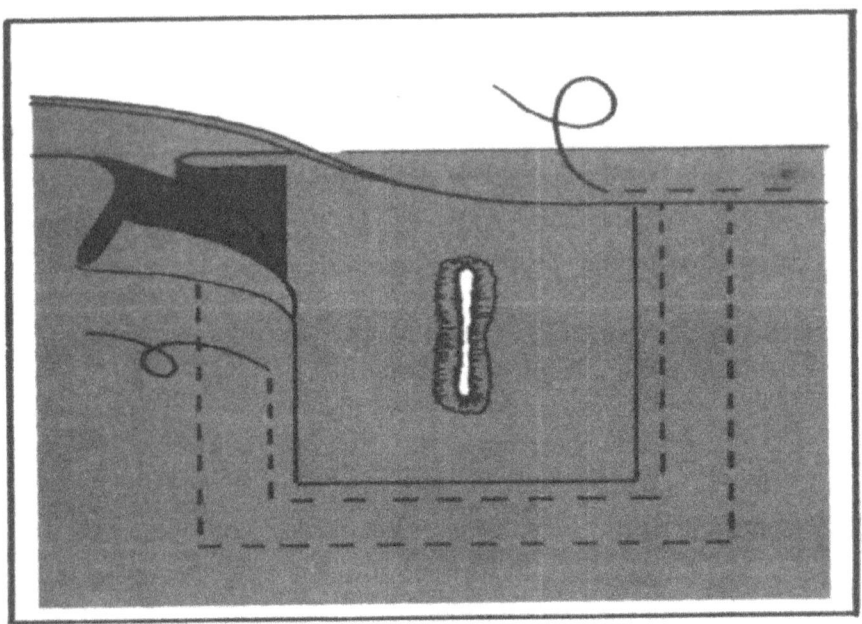

Figure 9-18. Felled patch method

Backing Method

9-31. To replace a buttonhole using the backing method (Figure 9-19)—

- Cut a strip of matching canvas wide enough to cover the damaged buttonhole and extend from the edge of the opening to 1-inch beyond the buttonhole. Allow ½ inch on each side for a turn under. Make the strip long enough to cover all the damaged buttonholes and extend 1 ½ inches above and below the buttonholes.
- Turn the strip of canvas face up.
- Draw chalk lines ½ inch from the raw edges on all sides.
- Turn the raw edges under on the chalk lines and crease the folded edges in place with the handle of a pair of shears.
- Turn the canvas item face down.
- Cover the damaged buttonholes with the canvas strip.
- Stitch the strip to the canvas item by sewing a seam ⅛ inch from the folded edges on all sides.
- Rework the buttonholes. Make slits for the buttonholes in the same place as the previous buttonholes. Reinforce the edges by stitching around the slits using the buttonhole stitch. Stitch through all layers.

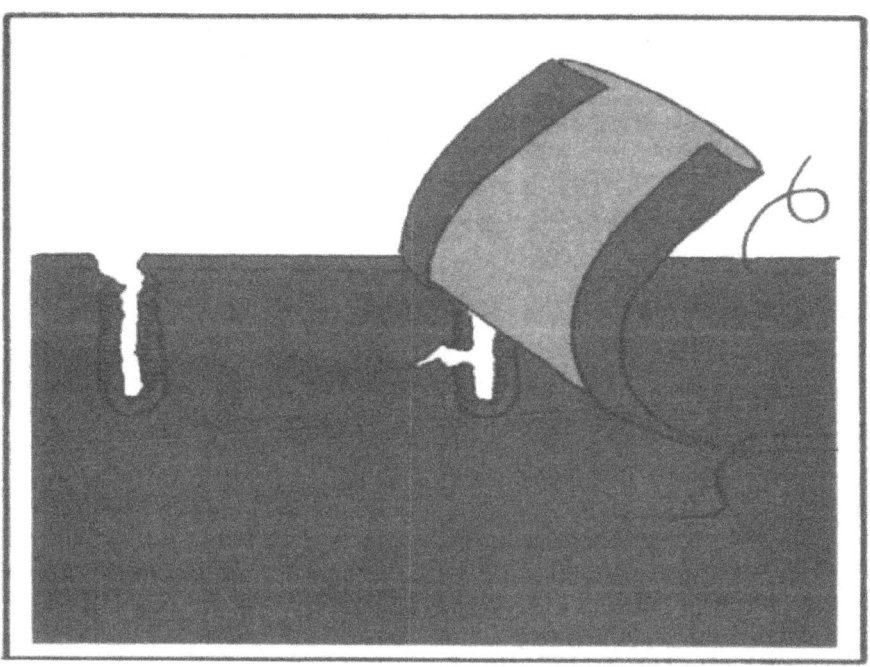

Figure 9-19. Backing method

New Facing & Backing Method

9-32. To make a buttonhole using the new facing and backing method—

- Cut away the damaged area.
- Draw chalk lines 1 inch from the raw edges.
- Cut a new facing and a new backing from matching canvas. Make both the facing and the backing large enough to extend ½ inch beyond the cutout area on three sides and 1 ½ inches on the side that will be attached to the canvas item or tent.
- Turn the facing and the backing face up. Draw chalk lines ½ inch from the raw edges on all sides.
- Turn under the raw edges along the chalk lines and crease the folded edges in place with the handle of a pair of shears.
- Turn the backing face down.
- Place the edge of the canvas item or tent face up on top of the backing so that the edge overlaps the backing by 1 inch. Use the chalk lines on the canvas item or tent as guidelines.
- Place the facing face up on top of the backing. Align all folded edges.
- Sew the facing and the backing to the canvas item or tent by stitching a seam around all four sides ⅛ inch from the folded edges.

119

- Make new buttonholes by cutting slits in the facing and the backing in the same places as the previous buttonholes and reinforcing the raw edges with the buttonhole stitch.

SECTION VI – Replacing Zippers

9-33. Damaged zippers are removed, and new or salvaged zippers are sewn in place the same way the original zipper was sewn in place. To replace the zipper of a general-purpose medium or large tent—

- Obtain a new or salvaged zipper the same color and length as the damaged one. Remember that a zipper is called a slide fastener in supply catalogs.
- Turn the tent inside out. Position the section with the damaged zipper face down on a worktable.
- Place the new zipper face down on top of the damaged zipper.
- Draw several horizontal chalk marks on each side of the new zipper (Figure 9-20). Draw the lines across the zipper tapes and the canvas in the tent. Use these index marks as guides to position the new zipper.
- Cut and remove the stitches holding the damaged zipper in place. Clean away all the loose threads.
- Unzip the new or salvaged zipper.
- Align the chalk marks on one side of the zipper with the chalk marks on the tent.
- Fold under the zipper tape $\frac{1}{2}$ inch the length of the zipper.
- Tack the beginning of the seam.
- Sew a seam 3/16 inch from the folded edge of the zipper (Figure 9-21). Sew to the eave of the tent, and tack the seam with a 1 inch tack.
- Sew a second seam $\frac{1}{4}$ inch from the first one. Tack the seam at the beginning and at the end.
- Repeat steps 7 through 11 above to sew the other side of the zipper in place.

Figure 9-20. Index marks for positioning new zipper

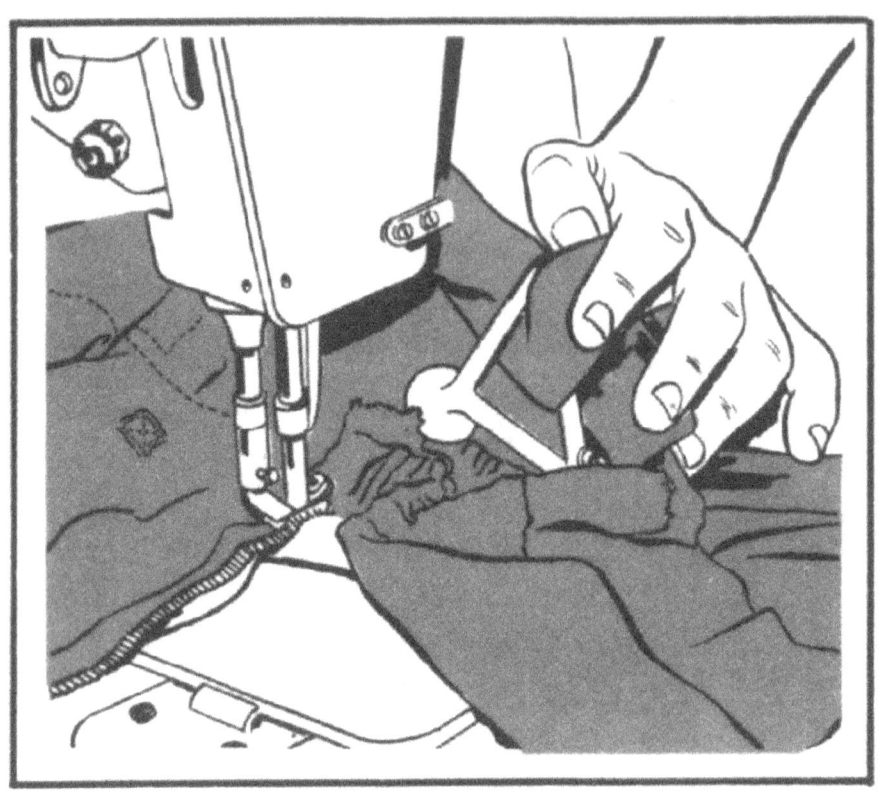
Figure 9-21. Sewing new zipper in place

CHAPTER 10 - REPAIRING WITH CEMENT AND SEALER

SECTION I – Minor Repairs

10-1. It is not always possible or practical to make sewn repairs on a tent. This is especially true when a tent is erect and the damage is minor. If a hole or tear is fairly small and it is not located near a seam, an edge, or hardware, a cemented patch or dab of adhesive can be used to repair the damage. When a stovepipe shield is slightly damaged, sealer can be used to repair the damage.

SECTION II – Cemented Repairs

10-2. The kind of cemented repair is determined by the size of the holes and tears. Repairs for holes and tears are described below.

Repairs for Small Holes

10-3. A dab of adhesive is used on a hole in a tent that measures $\frac{1}{8}$ inch or less across. To seal such a small hole (Figure 10-1)—

- Obtain a can of tent-patching adhesive, a wire brush, and a small stick or paddle.
- Use the wire brush to clean the area around the hole and raise the nap of the canvas.
- Use the small stick or paddle to put a dab of adhesive on the hole.
- Use the stick or paddle to work the adhesive into the canvas immediately. Bridge the hole with adhesive to seal it.

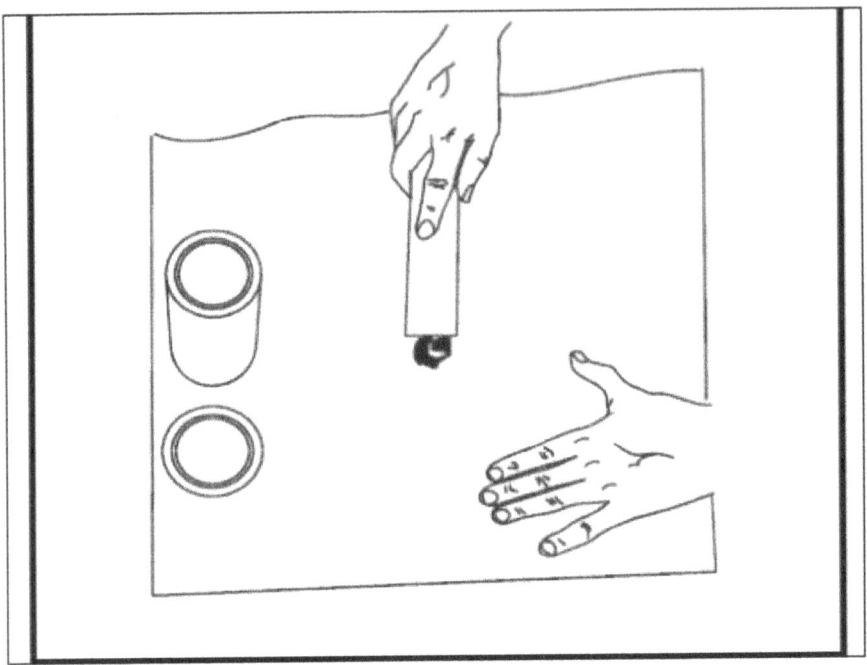

Figure 10-1. Cementing a small hole with adhesive

Repair for Large Holes & Tears

10-4. Cemented patches are used to cover holes and tears that are more than ⅛ inch but less than 4 ¾ inches across. Putting a cemented patch on a tent is similar to patching a bicycle tire. To apply a cemented patch (Figure 10-2)—

- Obtain a ruler, chalk, wire brush, flat board, paddle, roller, tent-patching adhesive, and a piece of clean matching canvas.
- Measure the damage.
- Cut a round patch from a piece of matching canvas. Make the patch large enough to extend ¾ inch beyond the damage in all directions.
- Place the board under the damage. (On an erect tent, another fabric repair specialist inside the tent holds the board against the damage.)
- Center the patch over the damage and draw a circle with chalk around the patch.
- Remove the patch. Use a wire brush to clean the canvas inside the circle and raise the nap of the canvas.
- Clean the patch with a wire brush.
- Place the patch face down over the damage.

124

- Open the can of adhesive and use the paddle to coat the patch evenly with adhesive. Let the adhesive overlap the edge of the patch a little so that it forms a circle on the tent.

CAUTION: *Seam sealer and solvent are extremely flammable and the fumes toxic. Do not smoke or use seam sealers or solvent near an open flame. Use seam sealer and solvent with goggles and gloves, and indoors with respirator or in an open, well ventilated area, away from sources of combustion. Death or severe injury may result from explosion or fire. Inhalation of fumes may cause toxic sickness. Do not leave the can open for long periods. Adhesive dries quickly.*

- Remove the patch. Flatten out the canvas and the edges of the hole or tear as much as possible. Fill in the circle with a coating of adhesive.
- Let the adhesive dry.
- Apply a second coat of adhesive to the tent and to the patch. Wait 10 or 15 minutes for the adhesive to become tacky. Test the patch by touching it. The patch is ready to use when it is sticky.
- Center the patch face up on top of the damage. Press the two sticky surfaces together.
- Use a roller to press the excess adhesive and the air bubbles from under the patch. Roll first in one direction and then in the opposite direction. If no roller is available, use the can of adhesive as a roller. First, tightly seal the can. Then tip it over on its side so that it will roll.
- Dip the top of one finger in the adhesive. Run the finger along the edge of the patch to seal the edge with an adhesive and prevent the edge from fraying.

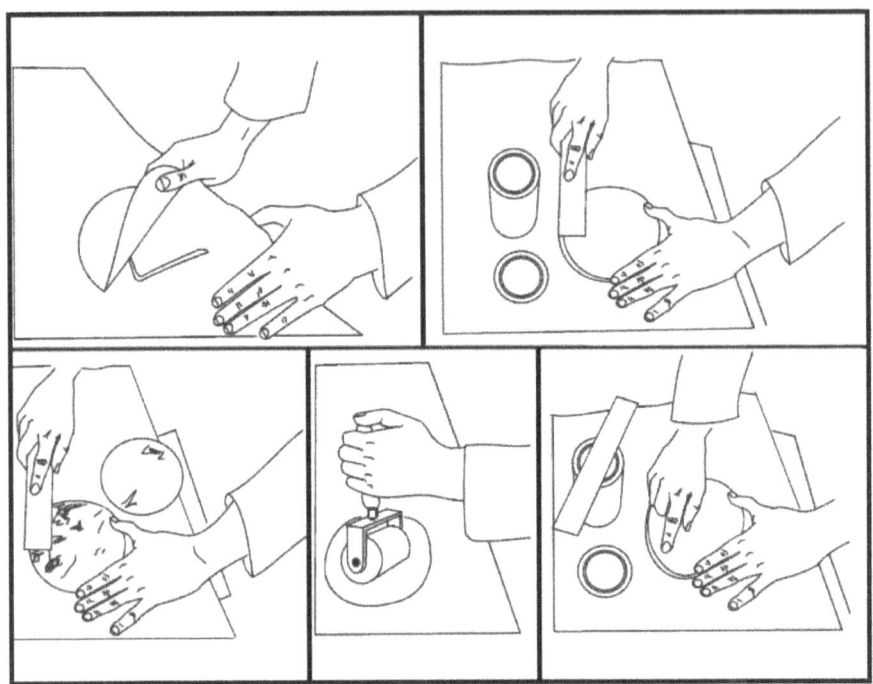

Figure 10-2. Cement patching a large hole

SECTION III – Sealer Repairs

10-5. Holes and tears in stovepipe shields can be repaired with a sealer. The kind of repair used depends on the extent of the damage, as described below.

Repairs for Small Holes & Tears

10-6. A layer of silicone sealer is used to repair a hole or tear that measure 2 inches or less across. To make this repair (Figure 10-3) —

- Obtain cleaning materials, a dry rag, a can of silicone sealer (MIL-A-46106), and a paddle.
- Clean and dry the damaged area thoroughly.
- Spread a 1/16 inch thick layer of sealer on both sides of the shield. Cover the hole or tear and at least ½ inch on each side of the damage. Smooth out the layer as evenly as possible.
- Brace the shield so that the sealer does not touch anything while it is wet.
- Let the sealer dry for 4 hours on a sunny day with low humidity. Let it dry for 6 hours on a humid day. Do not move the tent while the sealer is drying.

126

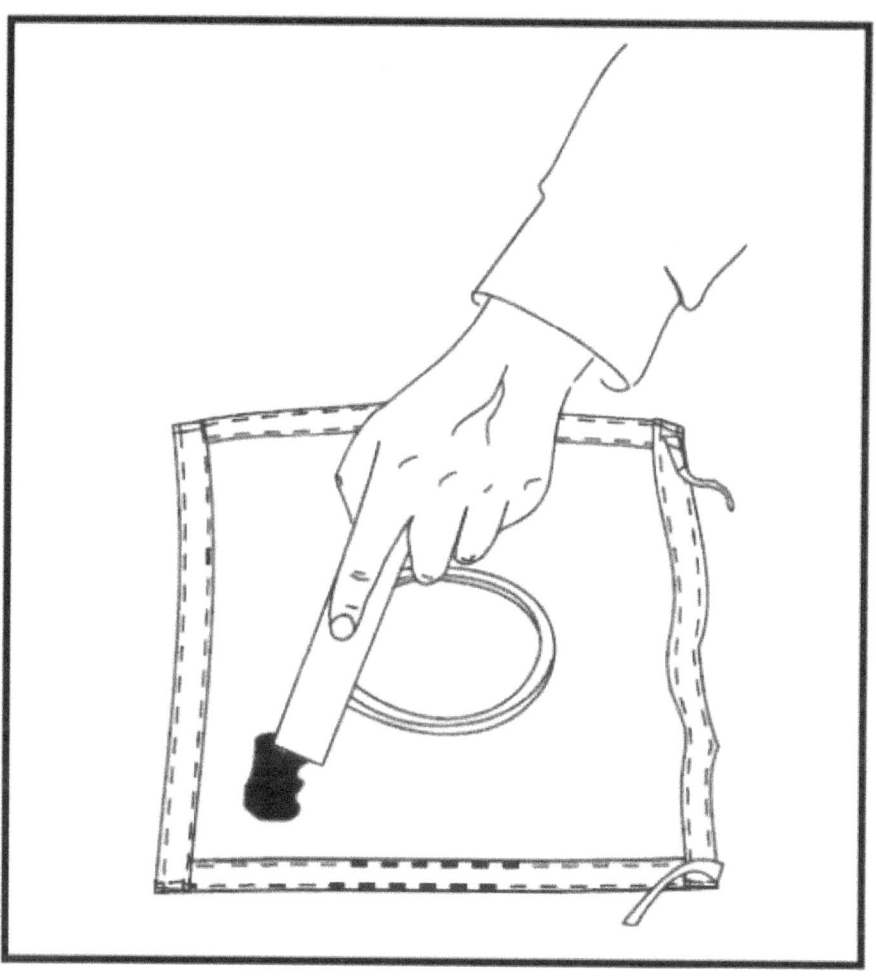

Figure 10-3. Using sealer to repair a small hole

Repairs for Large Holes & Tears

10-7. A patch attached with silicone sealer is used to repair holes and tears more than 2 inches across in stovepipe shields. To make this repair (Figure 10-4)—

- Obtain a ruler, cleaning materials, a dry rag, a craftsman's knife, a piece of matching patch material, a can of silicone sealer, and a paddle.
- Clean and dry the damaged area thoroughly.
- Measure the damaged area.
- Cut a patch from material salvaged from a shield that could not be repaired. Make the patch large enough to extend 1 inch beyond the damage on all sides.
- Spread a layer of sealer on either the patch or the shield.

127

- Press the patch in place at once.
- Spread sealer on the edges of the patch to 1 inch beyond the edges of the patch on all sides. Do not move the shield for 4 to 6 hours.

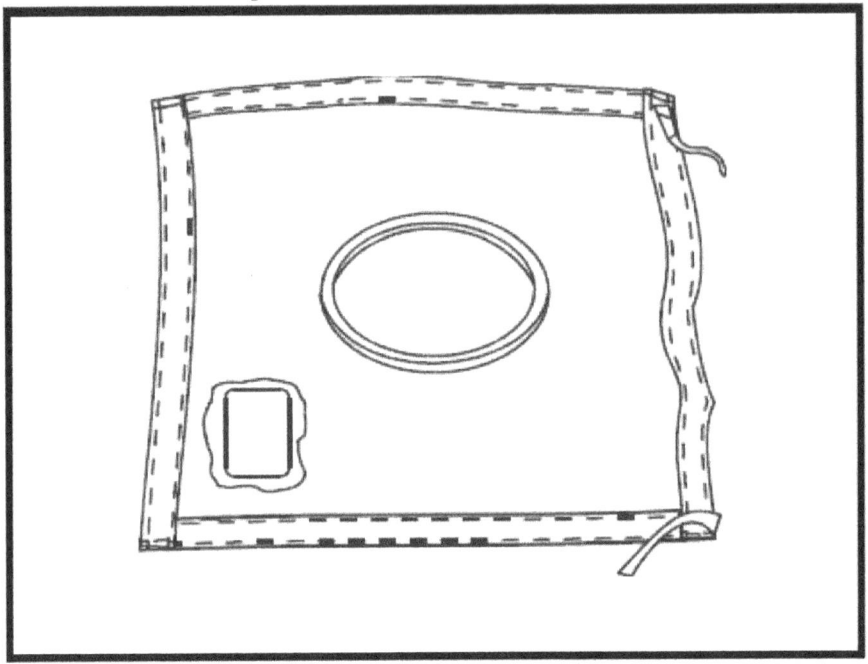

Figure 10-4. Using sealer to repair a large hole

ENVIRONMENTAL NOTE: *The Army environmental vision is to be a national leader in environmental and natural resources stewardship for present and future generations as an integral part of its mission. The Army must take care of the environment; that is, practice environmental stewardship. All operations conducted on Army installations will comply with federal, state, local and host-nation environmental requirements and Army regulations. The Army will sustain compliance at all sites in the US and abroad, establishing good relationships with communities and regulators. See TC 3-34.489 for additional information on the Army's environmental strategy and responsibilities.*

CHAPTER 11 - REPAIRING LINES

SECTION I – Types of Lines

11-1. Lines are ropes used on canvas and webbed items. Lines are made of nylon or natural fibers, such as manila, sisal, hemp, cotton, and jute. Nylon rope is about three times stronger than manila, the strongest natural rope fiber. Nylon is waterproof and it can stretch, absorb shocks, and return to its original size. It also resists wear, rot, and mildew. Lines made from natural fibers are treated to make them mildew resistant and water-repellant. Lines that become badly worn, frayed, or mildewed are replaced with new lines. New lines should be serviceable and the proper length. Knots and splices are used to attach lines to tents and canvas items. The knots and splices used to fasten new lines should be identical to those used on the original lines. They should be neatly done and the proper size.

SECTION II – Knots & Splices

11-2. Detailed instructions for making knots and splices are in TM 3-34.86. A variety of knots and splices are used in canvas and webbing repair.

Overhand Knot

11-3. The overhand knot (Figure 11-1) is the easiest knot to make and the most frequently used knot. It is used to keep the end of a tent line from slipping through the center of the grommet.

Footstop for a Single Grommet Fastening

11-4. A footstop for a single-grommet fastening (Figure 11-1), is a loop in a line that slips over a footstop pin at the bottom of a tent. It is formed by tying the two ends of a footstop line in a single overhand knot.

Footstop for a Two-Grommet Fastening

11-5. A footstop for a two-grommet fastening is formed by tying an overhand knot, (Figure 11-1), at each end of a footstop line.

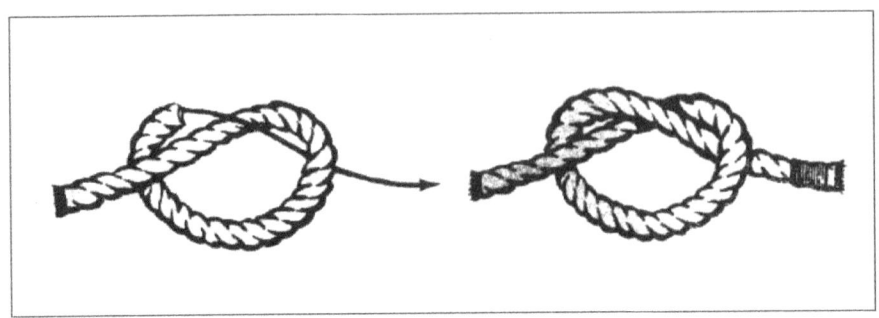

Figure 11-1. Overhand knot

Figure-Eight knot

11-6. The figure-eight knot (Figure 11-2) forms a larger knot at the end of a line than an overhand knot. It is used to keep a line from slipping through the center of a grommet or a loop in another line.

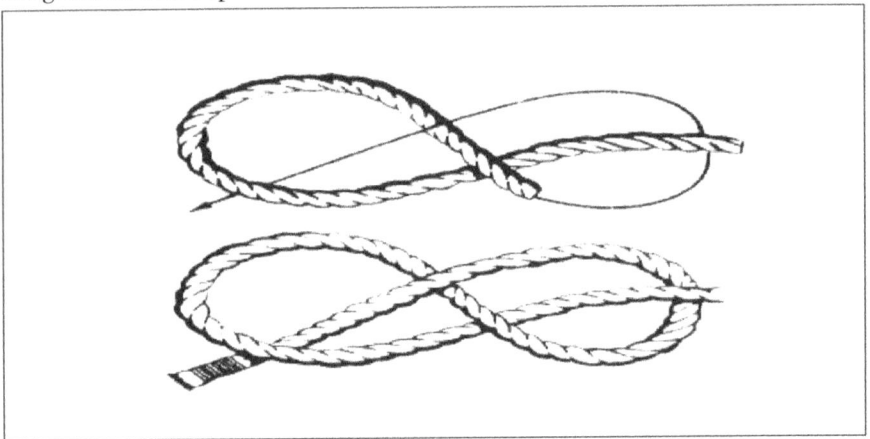

Figure 11-2. Figure-eight knot

Bowline Knot

11-7. The bowline knot (Figure 11-3) is used to form a loop that will not tighten or slip under strain, yet will untie easily.

130

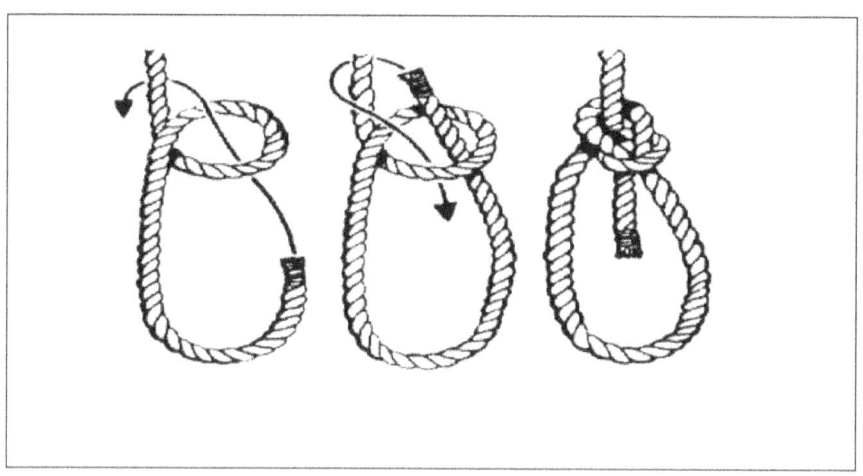

Figure 11-3. Bowline knot

Regular Eye Splice

11-8. A regular eye splice (Figure 11-4) is used to make a permanent loop at the end of a line. A regular eye splice is made by untwisting the strands at the end of the line and interweaving them with the strands in another part of the line.

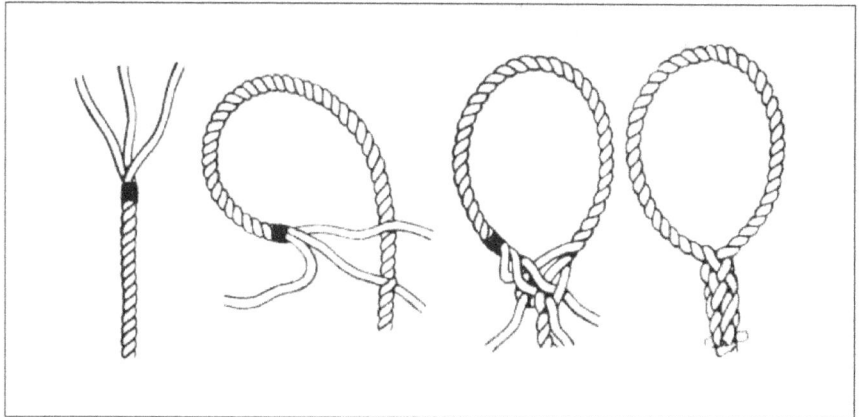

Figure 11-4. Regular eye splice

Sailmaker's Eye Splice

11-9. A sailmaker's eye splice (Figure 11-5) is used to make a loop that is going to be sewn to canvas. It is like a regular eye splice but the strands are interwoven so that they follow the lay of the line.

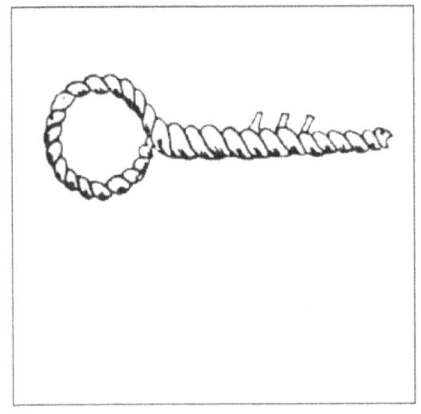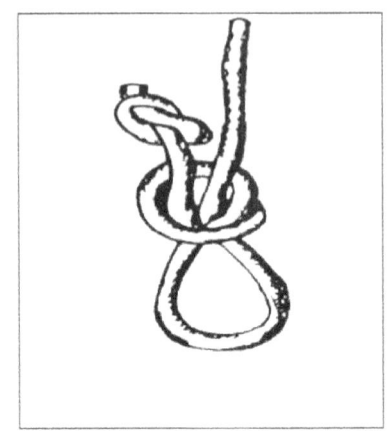

Figure 11-5. Sailmaker's Eye Splice and Tied Eye

Tied Eye

11-10. A tied eye (Figure 11-6) is a loop that is tied rather than spliced at the end of a line.

Short Splice

11-11. A short splice (Figure 11-7) is the strongest way to join two lines. Unlike the long splice, it increases the diameter of the line so that it may not be able to pass through rings, grommets, and other tent hardware. A short splice is made by untwisting a short section at the end of two lines and interweaving the strands so that they form one line.

Long Splice

11-12. A long splice (Figure 11-8) is another way to join two lines. Although it is weaker than a short splice and uses more line, it does not add much to the diameter of the line. The long splice can usually pass through rings, grommets, and other tent hardware.

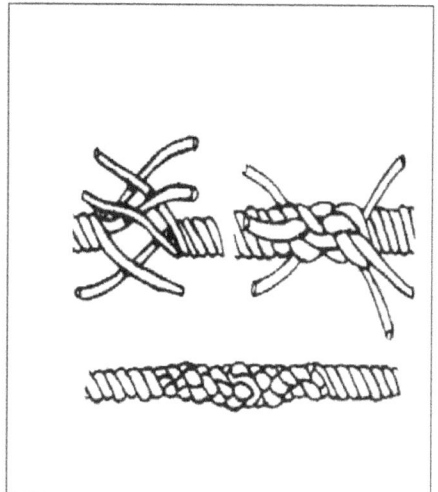 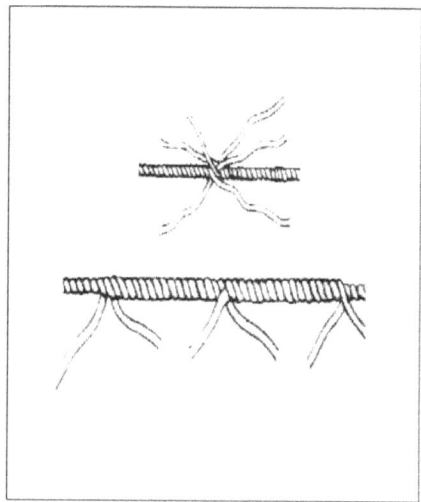

Figure 11-6. Short Splice and Long Splice

Cut Splice

11-13. A cut splice (Figure 11-9) is used to form an eye when two lines are joined. It is used on a double guy line. The pole spindle passes through the eye. The cut splice is formed by overlapping two lines, untwining the ends, and interweaving the strands.

Tied Cut

11-14. The tied cut (Figure 11-10) is used to join two cotton, braided lines.

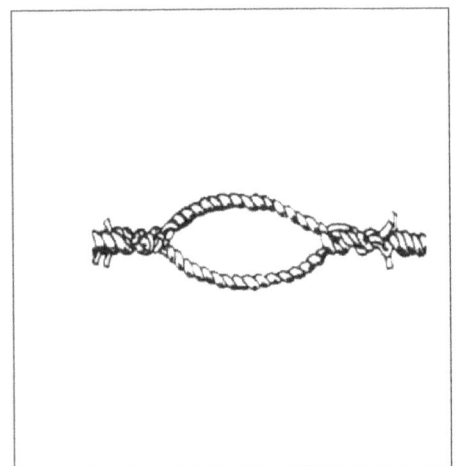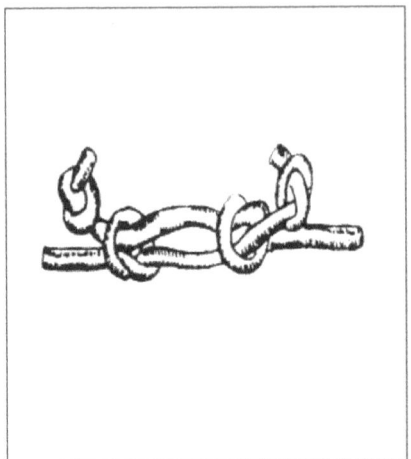

Figure 11-7. Cut Splice and Tied Cut

Whipped Rope End

11-15. Whipping (Figure 11-8) is wrapping the end of a line with cord to keep the line from unraveling. The cord is wrapped to the end of the line in the opposite direction of the lay of the line.

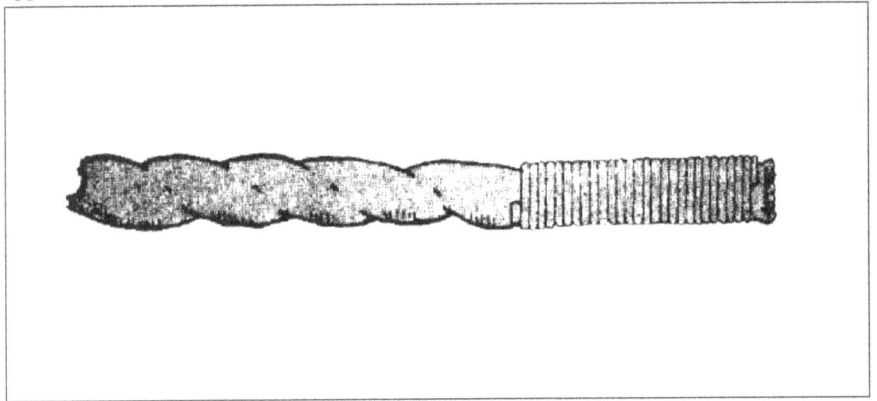

Figure 11-8. Whipped rope end

CHAPTER 12 - REPLACING HARDWARE

SECTION I – Attaching Hardware

12-1. Hardware is the metal equipment attached to a canvas or webbed item. Tack-buttons, grommets, snap fasteners, end clips, and rivets are fastened directly to the cloth. Some hardware, such as tent line slips, is attached directly to lines and poles. Other hardware is attached to tents and other items by means of canvas or webbing loops called chapes. When hardware is missing, broken, bent, cracked, rusted, or damaged in any other way, it is replaced with new or salvaged hardware.

12-2. Often it is necessary to darn, patch, or replace the supporting canvas. Newly attached hardware should be in good condition, properly positioned, and securely fastened to the canvas or webbed item. Fabric repair specialists should be familiar with all the hardware described in Table 12-1 and shown in Figure 12-1. Directions for attaching tack buttons, grommets, snap fasteners, end clips, rivets, and tent line slips are given in this chapter.

Item	Description
1. Rings	Round metal pieces used to fasten tie tapes, catch snap hooks, and support hand worked grommets
2. Loops	Elongated metal pieces used to hold webbing straps and to support hand worked grommets
3. Rings	D-shaped metal pieces used to catch snap hooks and loop over pole spindles on tents
4. Triangles	Triangular metal attachments used to ease the strain on canvas at pole spindles
5. Links	Metal pieces similar to chain links used at points where pole spindles pass through tent eaves and also used over pole spindles to support eave lines
6. Squares	Square metal pieces used with webbing
7. Double hooks	Metal pieces with two hooks used to attach canvas equipment to the individual equipment belt
8. Slide loops	Rectangular metal pieces with center bars used to adjust straps
9. Snap hooks	Metal hooks with spring-steel snaps used to catch numerous pieces of hardware
10. Wall D-rings	Fan-shaped D-rings used on assembly tents
11. S-hooks	S-shaped hooks used to catch rings and other pieces of hardware
12. Triangle with hooks	Triangular-hooked metal pieces used to connect fair-leads to webbing supports of tents
13. Fairleads	Magnesium metal casings used to keep eave lines from rubbing the canvas at tent eaves
14. 15., 16., Buckles	Metal fasteners used on strap ends
17. Sliding keepers	Metal pieces with slots used to hold straps in place

Table 12-1. Hardware items

Item	Description
18. Fasteners	Hooking metal devices used to fasten belt ends
19. Rope tips	Metal caps used to finish rope ends
20. Fastener supports	Metal, U-shaped pieces used to hold the male sections of style 1 snap fasteners
21. Ridge plates	Metal plates with holes used to protect and support the canvas around ridge pole spindles
22. Chains and plates	Metal plates with chains used at peaks on pyramid-shaped tents
23. Thimbles	Oval metal inserts which fit into splice eyes and are used to reinforce the ends of lines
24. Bull's eyes	Round wooden blocks with holes in the center used to carry hoisting lines
25. Staples	U-shaped metal pieces with finished ends which are riveted to cloth
26. Double washers	Metal pieces with holes in each end which are used to prevent staples from pulling through cloth
27. Shackle-type diamond eye hooks	Heavy steel wire hooks which have upper and lower shackles connected with bolts and nuts

Table 12-1. Hardware items cont.

136

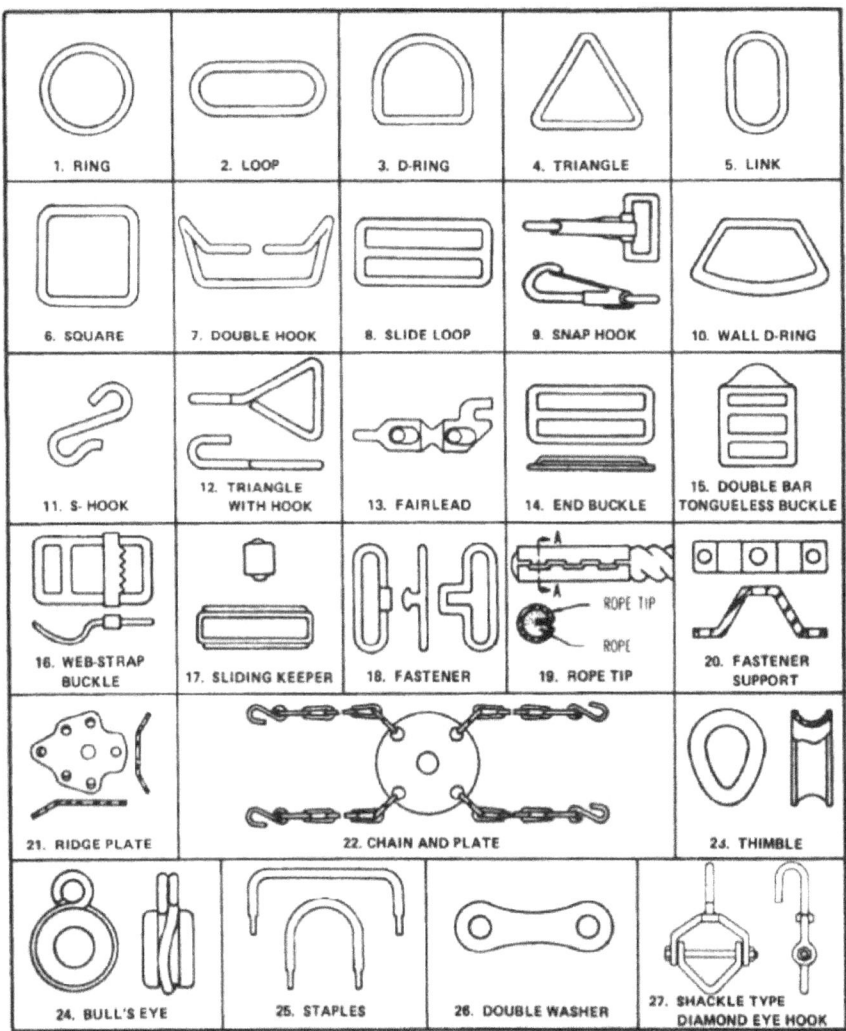

Figure 12-1. Hardware pieces

Section II – Replacing Tack Buttons

12-3. A tack button (Figure 12-2) is a two-part button that is used to close openings on canvas and webbed items. It can be attached either by hand or by using a tack-button attaching machine (Figure 12-3). Both ways are described below.

Attaching By Hand

12-4. To hand fasten a tack-button

- Remove the damaged tack-button and repair the canvas or webbing.

137

- Mark the exact position of the tack-button with chalk.
- Place the canvas or webbed item face up on top of a smooth, hard surface.
- Push the tack through the chalk mark from the underside of the canvas or webbing.
- Tap the button lightly with a rawhide mallet hard enough to clinch the tack and button to the canvas or webbing without damaging the tack-button or cloth.

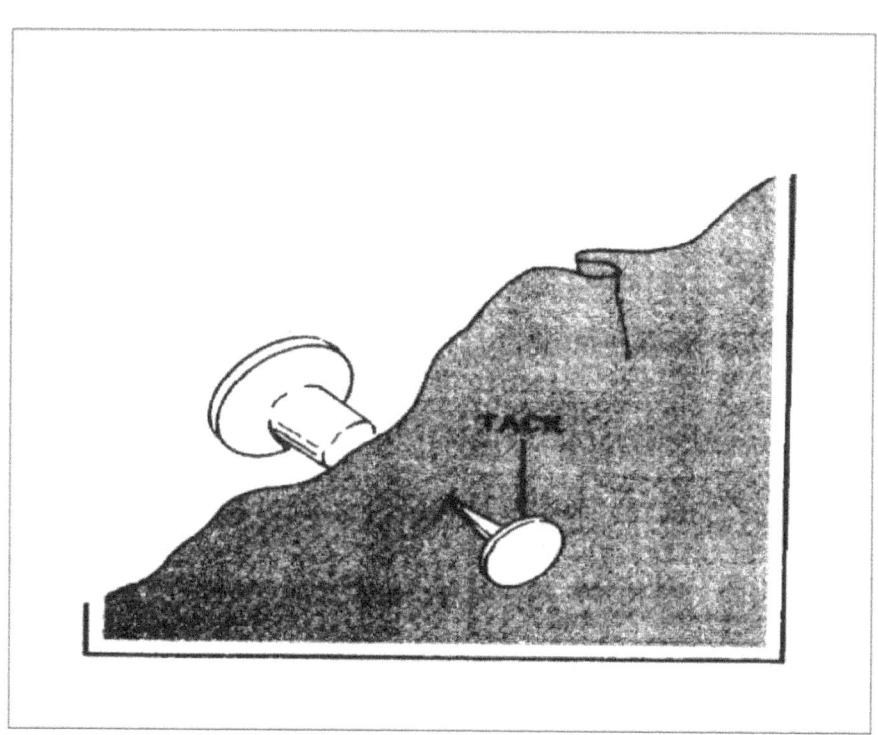

Figure 12-2. Tack-button

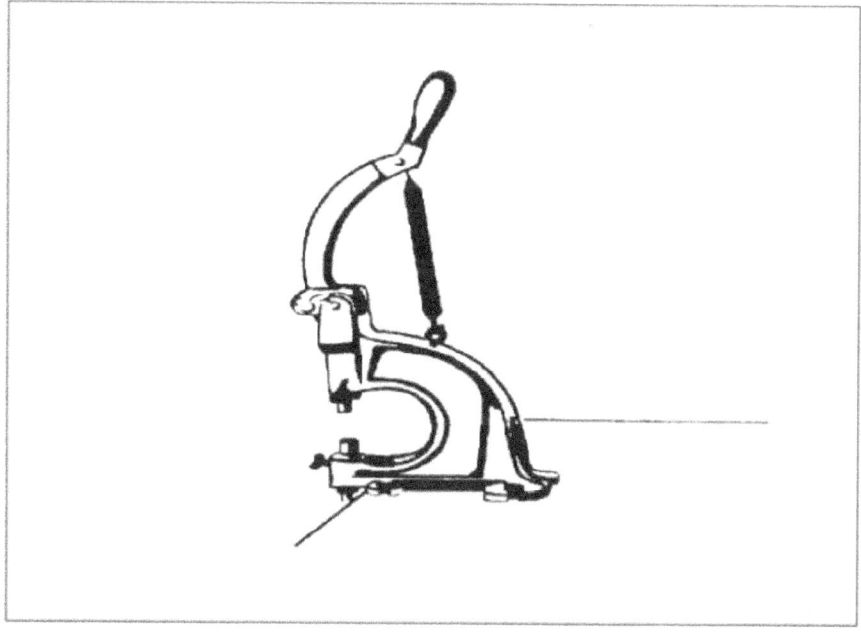

Figure 12-3. Tack-button attaching machine

Attaching by Machine

12-5. Detailed instructions for operating a tack-button attaching machine are given in TM 10-3530-207-14.

To machine fasten a tack-button-

- Remove the damaged tack-button and repair the canvas or webbing.
- Mark the exact position of the tack-button with chalk.
- Put the appropriate upper and lower die in the machine and adjust the pitch.
- Raise the hand lever and put the button into the upper die.
- Drop the tack, point up, into the lower die.
- Position the canvas or webbing face up over the lower die and tack.
- Press down the hand lever firmly to clinch the tack and button to the cloth.
- Raise the lever and remove the canvas or webbing item.
- Remove the die from the machine.

Section III – Replacing Grommets

12-6. Grommets are large metal eyelets or rings which are used to reinforce canvas and webbing where holes are made to hold ropes, lines, spindles, and webbed straps. If the canvas surrounding the grommet is damaged, it is repaired with a grommet-support patch before the grommet is replaced. In an emergency, the damaged grommet can be removed, and a larger grommet can be put in its place. This is done only when there is enough undamaged canvas to support the larger grommet adequately. Grommets are hand worked or die-inserted.

Hand Worked

12-7. A hand worked grommet is an iron ring sewn in place around a grommet hole. This type of grommet is often used in large tents because it can take a lot of strain. To hand work a grommet—

- If the old grommet will be used, obtain a rawhide mallet, sailmaker's needle, thread, wax, and an iron ring with an inside diameter larger than that of the hole. Also obtain a fid (a tapered, wooden, or metal pin).
- If a new grommet hole will be cut, obtain the tools listed above, a heavy woodblock, and a size 5 cutting punch for a ½ or ¾ inch ring or a size 6 cutting punch for a 1 inch ring. Position the canvas face up on the end grain surface of the woodblock and cut a grommet hole with the appropriate cutting punch (Figure 12-4).
- Center the ring over the grommet hole.
- To make stitching easier, use the sailmaker's needle to make a series of equally spaced holes about ⅛ inches from the outside

edge of the metal ring (Figure 12-5). Do not make the holes any larger than 1/16 inch across.

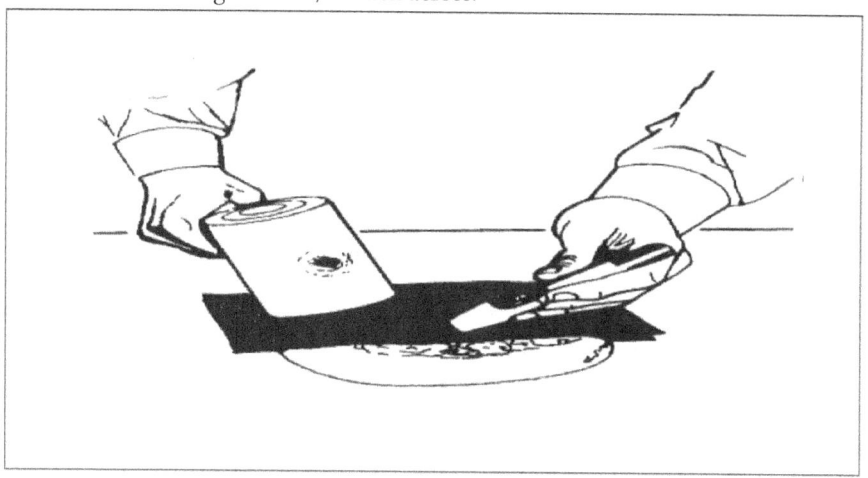

Figure 12-4. Cutting a grommet hole

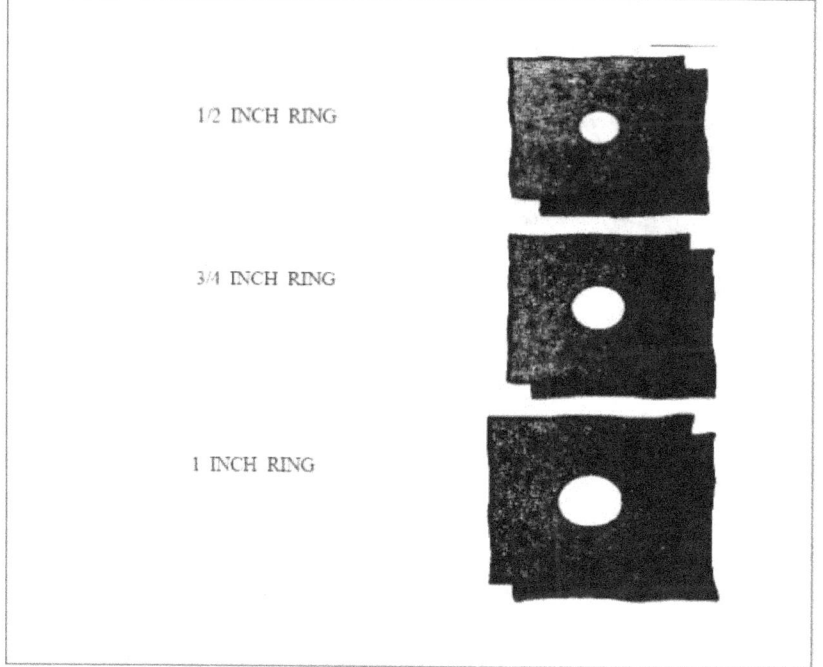

1/2 INCH RING

3/4 INCH RING

1 INCH RING

Figure 12-5. Series of equally spaced holes

- Thread the needle with four strands of waxed thread, and knot the ends. Twist the strands together, re-wax the thread, and cut off the knot.

141

- Stick the needle into one of the needle holes, and draw the thread through the hole until a ½ inch end is left.
- Hold the ½ inch length of thread down against the canvas and the edge of the ring with the free end pointing clockwise.
- Bring the needle up through the grommet hole, over the ring and the ½ inch end and stick it down into the next needle hole.
- Continue stitching clockwise, making a series of round stitches around the grommet hole (Figure 12-6).
- Finish the stitching by sticking the needle under the last two stitches and pulling the thread up tightly.
- Leave free a ½ inch length of thread and cut the thread.
- Flatten the stitching by pushing the fid into the grommet hole, first from one side and then the other.

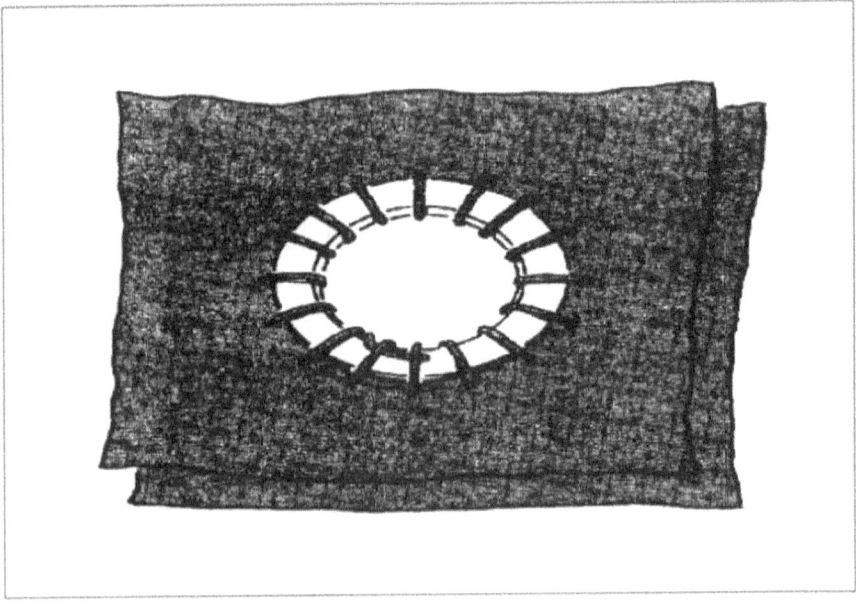

Figure 12-6. Series of round stitches around a grommet

Die-Inserted

12-8. A die-inserted grommet consists of two brass parts. The male half, called a barrel, is smooth. The female half, called a washer, has spurs that grip the canvas or webbing. Punch-and-die sets are used to clinch the two parts together. To insert a grommet—

- If the old grommet hole will be used, obtain a rawhide mallet, a brass grommet, and a punch and-die set. Use a size 4 punch-and-die set with a size 4 grommet and a size 5 punch-and-die set with a size 5-grommet.

- If a new grommet hole will be cut, obtain the tools listed above, a heavy woodblock, and a size 5 cutting punch for a size 4-grommet and a size 6 cutting punch for a size 5- grommet. Position the canvas face up on the end-grain surface of the woodblock and cut a grommet hole with the cutting punch.
- Insert the barrel into the hole through the underside of the canvas.
- Place the canvas and the flat bottom part of the barrel on the grommet die (Figure 12-7).
- Place the washer, spurs down, over the barrel.
- Insert the punch into the barrel, and hold the punch in place with one hand.
- Hit the top of the punch with a rawhide mallet hard enough to clinch the two parts to the canvas without damaging the grommet or the canvas (Figure 12-7). When the parts are clinched properly, the edge of the barrel has a smooth roll.

Figure 12-7. Placing barrel on grommet die and hitting punch with a rawhide mallet

SECTION IV – REPLACING SNAP FASTENERS

12-9. The two types of snap fasteners used to close openings on canvas and webbing are styles 1 and 2. Style 1 can be used on heavier canvas than style 2.

Style 1 Snap Fastener

12-10. A style 1 snap fastener has two sections, a female half and a male half. The female half has two parts; a socket and a clinch plate. The male half also has two parts; a stud and a washer. The stud is available in two sizes, single and double. The double stud is twice as long as the single stud and can hold an additional layer of canvas. To install a style 1 snap fastener (Figure 12-8)-

- Obtain a style 1 snap fastener, chalk, socket punch, socket anvil, hole punch, stud set, stud anvil, rawhide mallet, and lead block.

143

- Remove the old snap fastener and patch or replace the canvas if necessary.
- Mark with chalk the exact position of the hole for the female half of the snap fastener.
- Place the canvas over the lead block so that the chalk mark is centered on the block.
- Center the socket punch over the chalk mark.
- Hit the socket punch with a rawhide mallet to make slots for the socket prongs and a center hole.
- Insert the socket prongs into the slits through the underside of the canvas.
- Place the clinch plate over the socket prongs.
- Place the canvas and socket, prongs up, on the socket anvil.
- Bend the socket prongs toward the center with the top of the socket punch until the prongs are flat against the clinch plate and the plate and socket are securely clinched to the canvas.
- Mark the exact position of the hole for the male half of the snap fastener.
- Use a hole punch to make a hole a little smaller than the barrel of the stud so that the barrel will fit snugly into the hole.
- Insert the barrel of the stud up through the hole.
- Center the canvas and stud, with the barrel up, on the stud anvil.
- Place the washer over the barrel of the stud.
- Place the tip of the stud set in the barrel. Hold the stud set in place with one hand.
- Hit the top of the stud set with the rawhide mallet, securely clinching the stud and the washer to the canvas.

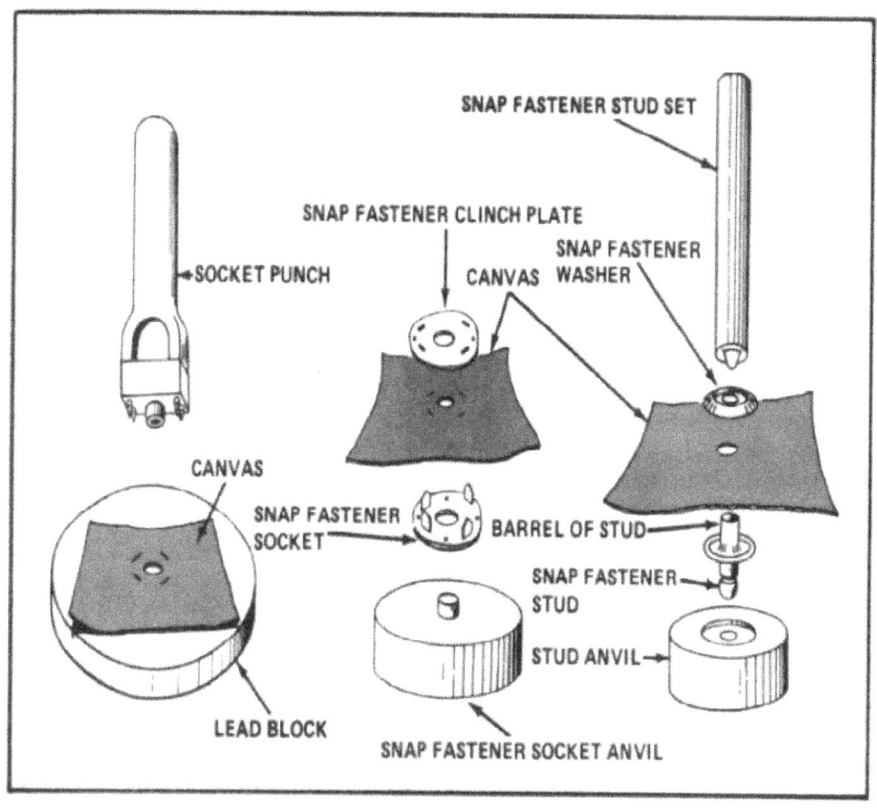

Figure 12-8. Replacing a type 1 snap fastener

Style 2 Snap Fastener

12-11. The style 2 snap fastener is identical to the snap fastener used on clothing. Paragraph 4-20 describes this style of snap fastener and how it is installed. Follow the same instructions to install a style 2 snap fastener on canvas and webbing but use a patch instead of a darn to repair the supporting canvas in a tent

SECTION V – ATTACHING END CLIPS

12-12. End clips are metal tips used to prevent the cut ends of webbing from unraveling. They also make it easier to insert webbing ends into grommets and buckles. The three types of end clips (Figure 12-9) are ball-type, flat-type, and end buckle.

Ball-Type End Clip

12-13. The ball-type end clip looks like a hollow metal ball before it is attached to webbing. It fits like a thimble over the end of the webbing. To attach this clip, stick the webbing into the clip, partially flatten the clip with a hammer, straighten the webbing, and finish flattening the clip.

Flat-Type End Clip

12-14. The flat-type end clip is a V-shaped strip of metal. The ends of the clip have teeth which grip the webbing. To attach this clip, stick the webbing into the jaws of the clip, and flatten the clip with a hammer.

End Buckle Clip

12-15. The end buckle clip is a flat-type end clip with a slot for a buckle or hook. It also has holes for riveting the clip in place after it has been flattened with a hammer.

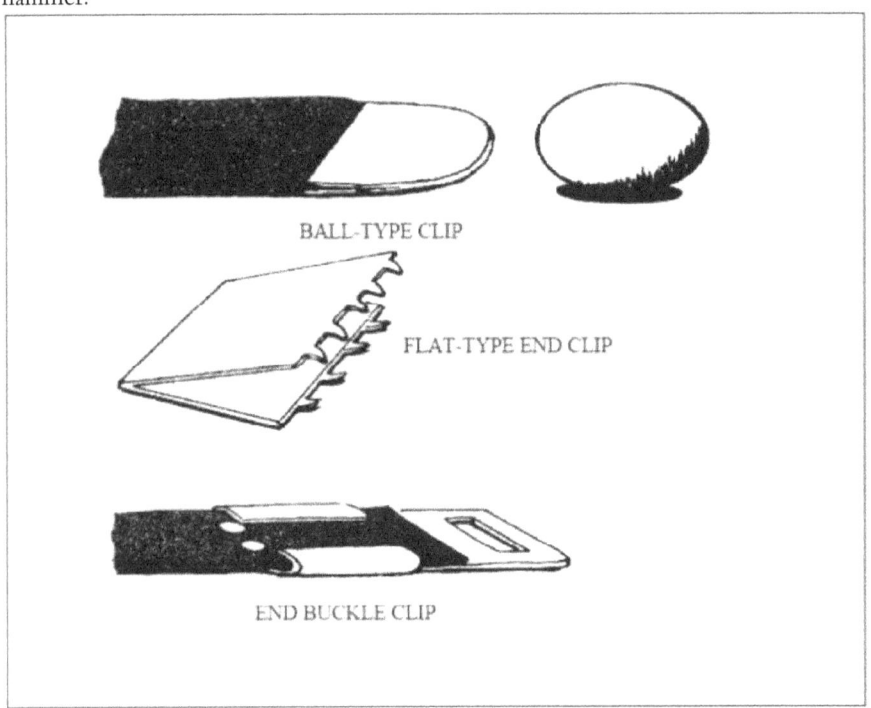

Figure 12-9. End clips

SECTION VI – INSTALLING RIVETS

12-16. Rivets are metal pins and heads which are used to hold two or more pieces of canvas together. The two types of rivets are belt and tubular. All rivets are installed by the same method.

Belt Rivets

12-17. Belt rivets (Figure 12-10) are made of solid brass or copper. They come in sizes 8, 10, 12, and 14, with lengths from ³⁄₈ to 1 ¹⁄₄ inches. The head of this type of rivet is called a burr. The burr size should match that of the rivet.

Tubular rivets

12-18. Tubular rivets (Figure 12-10) are made with hollow brass shanks. They come in 3/16 to ¾ inch lengths. The head of this rivet is called a cap. The end of a tubular rivet is beveled so that it will form a flange inside the rim of the cap.

Installation

12-19. To install a belt or tubular rivet—

- Use a hole punch to cut a hole in the layer or layers of canvas or webbing. Make the hole small enough to fit tightly around the rivet.
- Insert the rivet into the hole. Use a size of rivet that will pass through all the canvas or webbing with very little excess and still take a cap or burr.
- Place the canvas or webbing and the rivet, head down, on a metal block.
- Place the burr cap on the rivet.
- Clinch the burr and belt rivet together by hitting the burr with a ball peen hammer. Clinch the cap and tubular rivet together by hitting the cap with a plain-faced hammer.

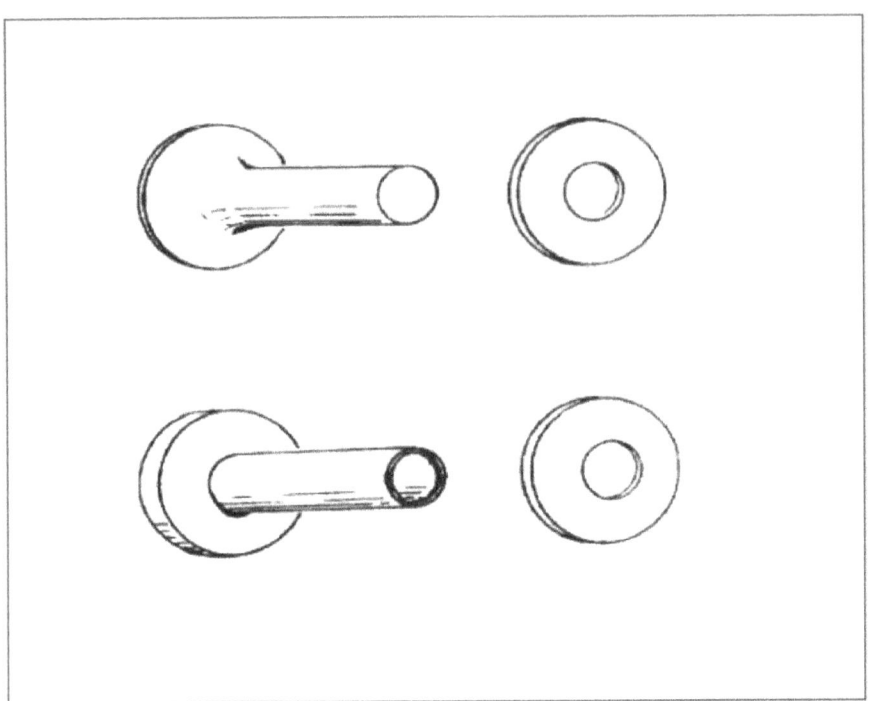

Figure 12-10. Rivets

SECTION VII – INSTALLING TENT LINE SLIPS

12-20. Tent line slips (Figure 12-11) are metal devices used to adjust eave and guy lines on a tent. There are four types of tent line slips. Wire Slip, Type I Quick-Release Flat Slip, Type II Barbell Slip, and Type III Flat Slip.

Wire Slip

12-21. A wire slip is 4 inches long and 3/16 inch wide. It is made of steel. One end is coiled like a spring and the other end is looped to form an eye. To install a wire slip—

- Pass one end of an eave line through the coil from the opening closest to the outside.
- Pull 2 feet of line through the coil.
- Pass the same end of the line through an eave grommet from the roof side to the wall side.
- Pass the same end of the line through the eye of the wire slip.
- Secure the slip to the line by tying an overhand knot in the end of the line.

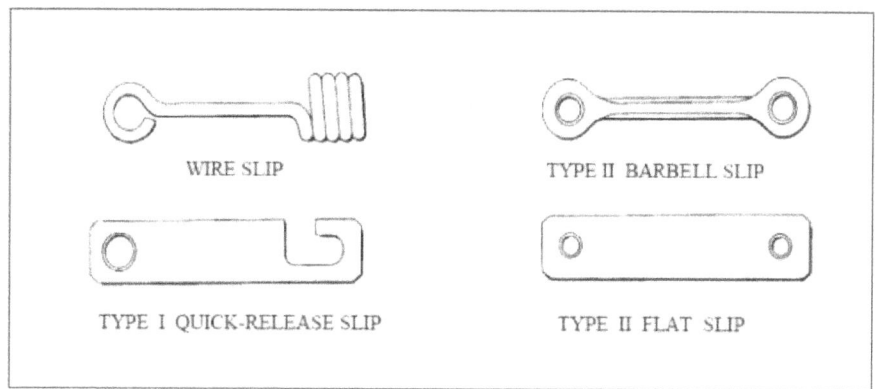

Figure 12-11. Tent line slips

Type I Quick-Release Flat Slip

12-22. This slip is 4 inches long and ⅞ inch wide. It is made of magnesium alloy. It has a round hole at one end and a quick-release side opening at the other end. To install a type I quick-release flat slip—

- Pass one end of an eave line through the hole in the slip.
- Pull 2 feet of line through the hole.
- Pass the same end of the line through an eave grommet from the roof side to the wall side.
- Pass the same end through the side opening at the other end of the slip.
- Secure the slip to the line by tying an overhand knot in the end of the line.

Type II barbell slip

12-23. This slip is 4 inches long and has a 7/16 inch wide hole at each end. It looks like a barbell. To install a type II barbell slip—

- Pass one end of an eave line through one of the holes in the slip.
- Pull 2 feet of line through the hole.
- Pass the same end of the line through an eave grommet from the roof side to the wall side.
- Pass the same end of the line through the other hole in the slip.
- Secure the slip to the line by tying an overhand knot in the end of the line.

Type III Flat Slip

12-24. This slip is similar to the quick-release flat slip but it has a hole at each end instead of a hole and a side opening. It is installed using the same method that is used to install a type II barbell slip.

CHAPTER 13 - REPAIRING WEBBING

SECTION I – Types of Webbing

13-1. Webbing is a strong band woven from nylon or cotton. It is used to construct the chapes, loops, billets, straps, and handles which are sewn to canvas items. Nylon webbing is waterproof and mildew-resistant. It also resists fraying and breaking. Repairs to nylon webbing usually involve re-stitching the webbing which has been pulled loose from the supporting canvas. Cotton webbing is treated to make it subject to wear because it is made of a natural fiber. Repairs to cotton webbing often involve replacing the entire webbing.

SECTION II – Chapes

13-2. Chapes (Figure 13-1) are folded and overlapped strips of canvas and webbing. They are used to attach hardware, such as buckles and rings, to tents and canvas items. Chapes are called D-rings, chapes, buckle-chapes, and other similar names, according to the hardware they carry. Damaged chapes are replaced with new chapes which are fitted and sewn in place using folds and seams identical to those used in the original construction of the item. Directions for fitting, sewing, and reinforcing chapes are given below.

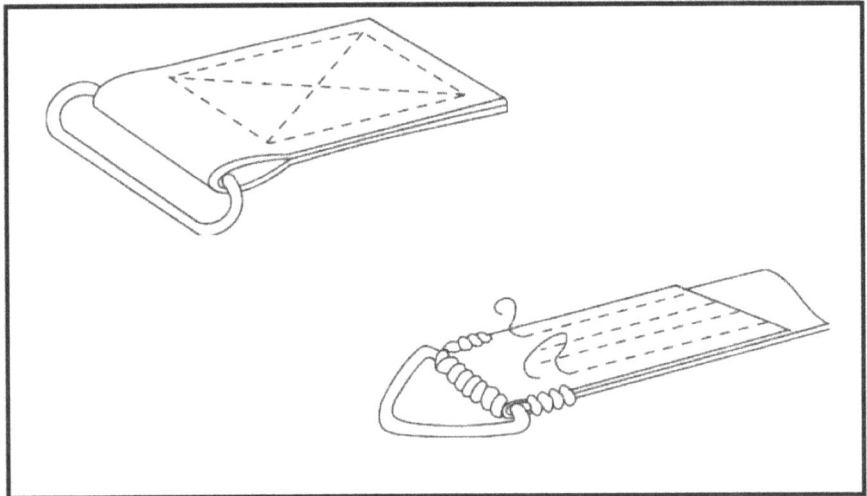

Figure 13-1. Chapes

Fitting

13-3. Webbing for chapes is folded and overlapped to fit a certain use or piece of hardware. Four types of folds are used to fit chapes.

150

Type 1 Fold

13-4. Type 1 fold (Figure 13-2) is made with a piece of webbing that is twice as long as the planned chape. To make a type 1 webbing fold--

- Fold the webbing in half and crease the fold flat.
- Insert one half of the webbing through the hardware.

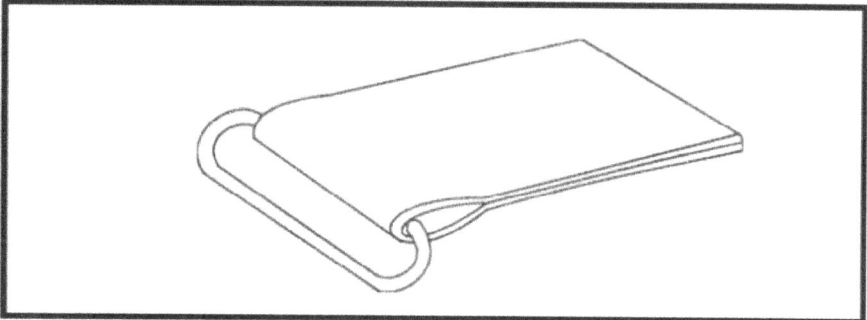

Figure 13-2. Type 1 fold

Type 2 Fold

13-5. For type 2 fold (Figure 13-3), the webbing is cut that it is twice as long as the planned chape. To make a type 2 webbing fold, insert one end of the webbing through the hardware, and then--

- Fold one end of the webbing under until it is 1 to 2 inches from the other end.
- Move the hardware until it lies in the fold.
- Fold under the other end of the webbing so that the two ends butt against one another.

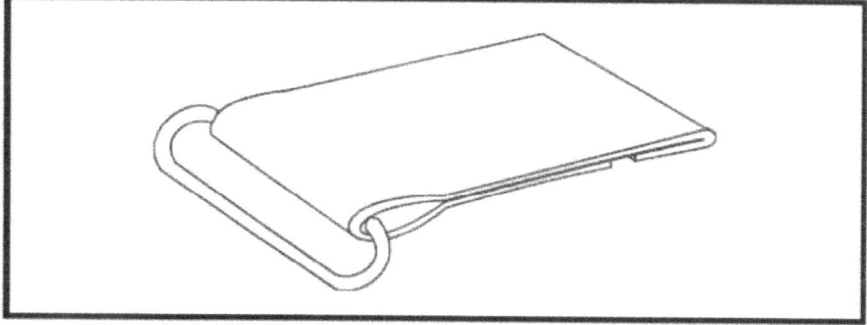

Figure 13-3. Type 2 fold

Type 3 Fold

13-6. Type 3 fold (Figure 13-4) is made with webbing 1 to 2 inches longer than twice the length of the planned chape. To make a type 3 webbing fold, place the hardware on the webbing, and then--

- Fold one end under until it is 1 to 2 inches from the other end. Slide the hardware on the webbing until it lies in the fold.
- Fold the other end of the webbing under so that the two ends overlap.

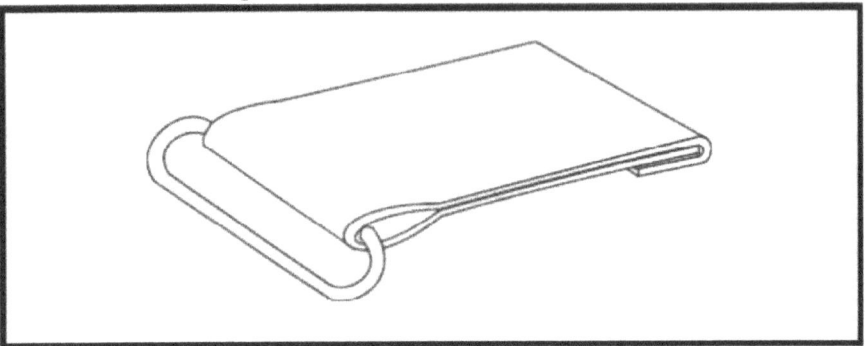

Figure 13-4. Type 3 fold

Type 4 Fold

13-7. Type 4 fold (Figure 13-5) is made by folding a piece of webbing that is four times as long as the planned chape. To make a type 4 webbing fold--
- Fold the webbing in half.
- Stick the folded end through the hardware.
- Fold the webbing in half again so that the first fold is on top and even with the two cut ends. Move the hardware so that it lies in the second fold.

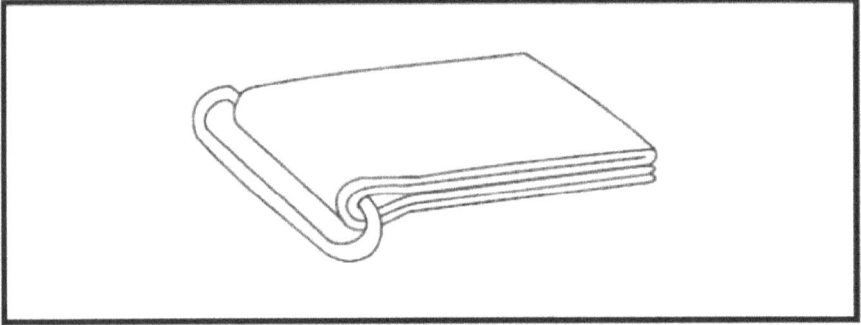

Figure 13-5. Type 4 fold

Sewing

13-8. Chapes are topstitched in place with an X-shaped seam (Figure 13-6). Webbing sewn in place with this type of stitching is less likely to pull loose. To sew a chape in place—
- Position the chape on top of the canvas item.

- Insert the chape and canvas under the presser foot of a heavy-duty sewing machine so that the hardware is to the left.
- Start stitching a seam in the upper right-hand corner ¼ inch from the edge. Tack the seam at the beginning.
- Stitch around the four sides of the chape in a clockwise direction. Pivot the chape and canvas on the needle at each corner.
- Pivot the chape and canvas on the needle and stitch diagonally across the chape from the upper right-hand corner to the lower left-hand corner.
- Pivot the chape and canvas on the needle. Stitch over the side seam to the upper left-hand corner.
- Pivot the chape and canvas on the needle. Stitch across the chape diagonally from the upper left-hand corner to the lower right-hand corner.
- Pivot the chape and canvas on the needle. Stitch over the side seam to the upper right-hand corner. Tack the seam at the end.

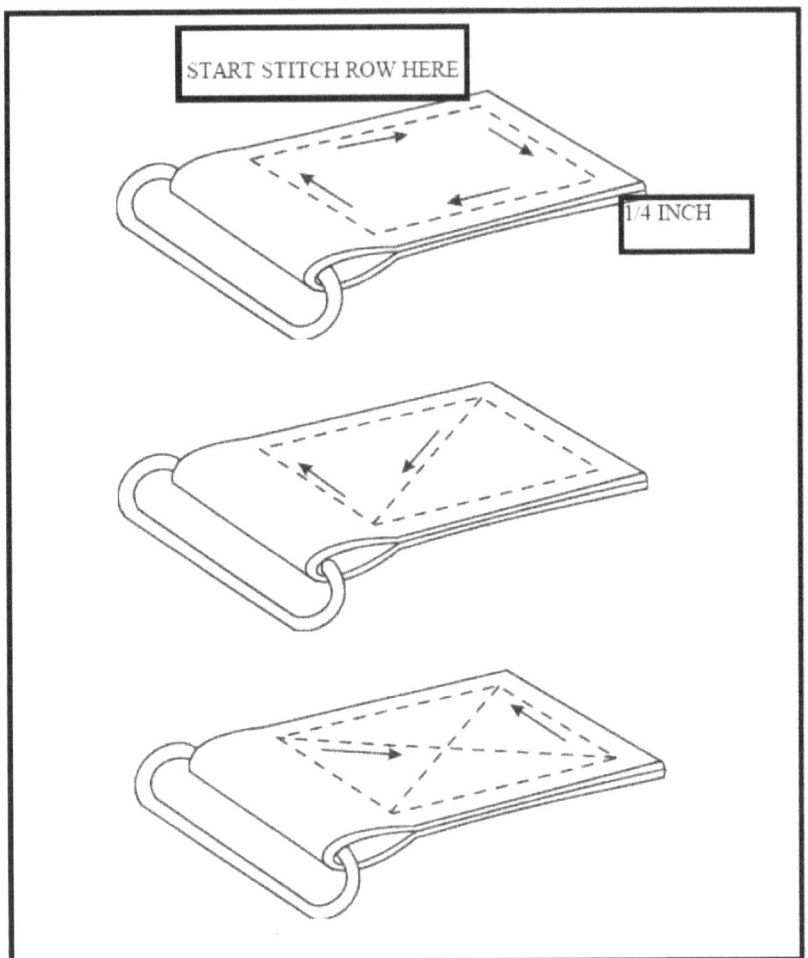

Figure 13-6. X-shaped chape seam

Reinforcing

13-9. Some chapes are subject to a lot of pulling and tugging. These chapes should be reinforced to prevent the underlying canvas from tearing. Use one of the following methods to reinforce chapes:

Webbing

13-10. Sew another piece of webbing across the chape as reinforcement (Figure 13-7). Sew the reinforcement in place the same way the chape was sewn in place.

154

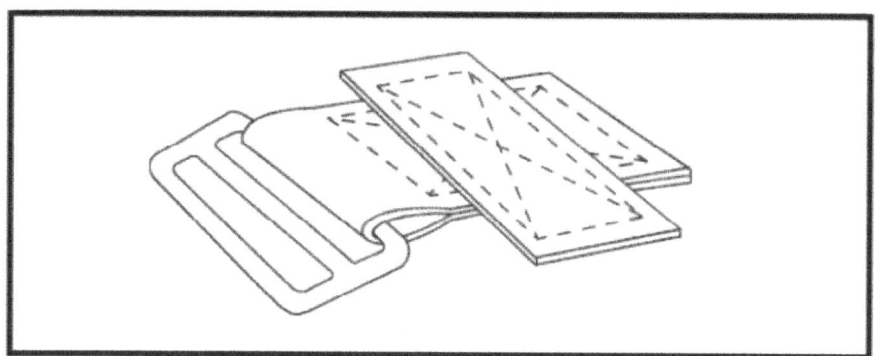

Figure 13-7. Reinforcement webbing

Stitching

13-11. Sew four parallel rows of machine stitching the length of the chape (Figure 13-8). Hand sew four round stitches on both sides of the looped end of the chape. Sew five round stitches on the end looped through the hardware.

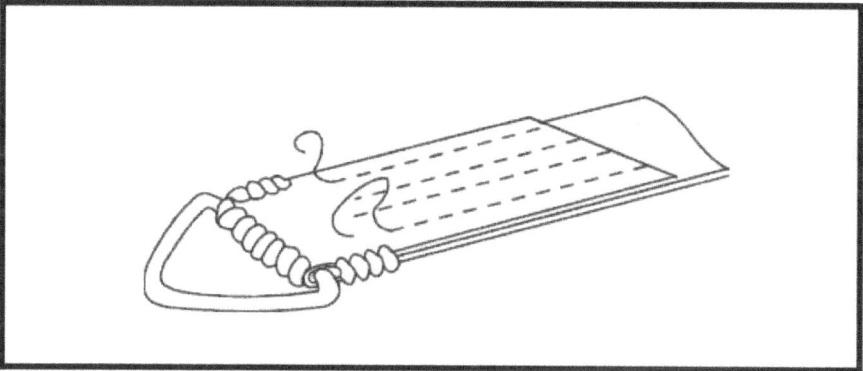

Figure 13-8. Reinforcement stitching

Section III – Loops

13-12. Loops are pieces of webbing which form openings when they are sewn to canvas items. They are used to hold and fasten lines and straps in place. Four kinds of loops can be made with webbing.

Flat Loop

13-13. The flat loop (Figure 13-9) lies entirely against the canvas item. To make a flat loop-

- Cut a piece of webbing the length of the planned loop plus enough to form a turn under at each end.
- Turn under the ends.
- Sew the webbing to the canvas item with X-shaped seams.

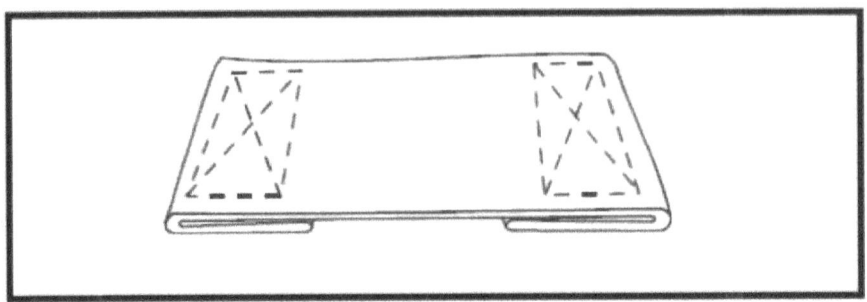

Figure 13-9. Flat loop

Short Loop

13-14. The short loop (Figure 13-10) sticks out a short distance from the canvas item. To make a short loop-

- Cut a piece of webbing. Allow for a short loop and the turn under at each end.
- Fold the webbing in half to form a little loop.
- Sew a seam across the webbing at the base of the loop.
- Turn under the ends.
- Sew the webbing to the canvas item with X-shaped seams.

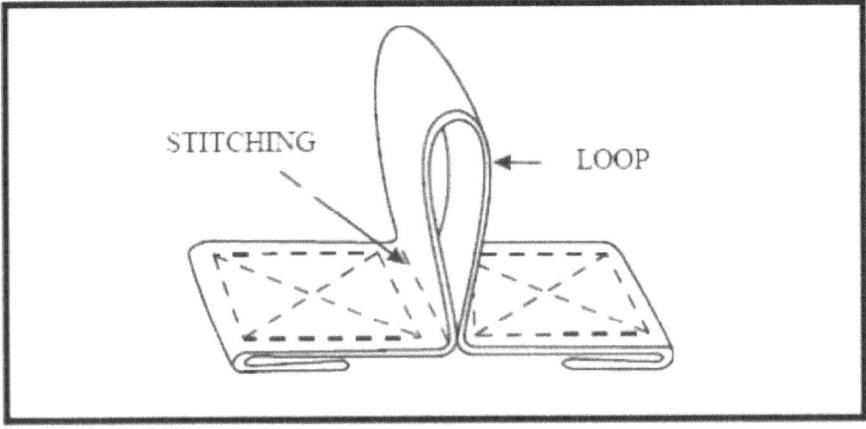

Figure 13-10. Short loop

Two-Ply Long Loop

13-15. The two-ply long loop (Figure 13-11) is used where a strong, lengthy loop is needed. To make this loop-

- Cut two pieces of webbing. Allow for a long loop and the turn under at each end.
- Sew the two pieces of webbing together with a row of stitches along each edge.

- Fold the webbing to form a long loop.
- Sew a seam across the webbing at the base of the loop.
- Turn under the ends.
- Sew the webbing to the canvas item with X-shaped seams.

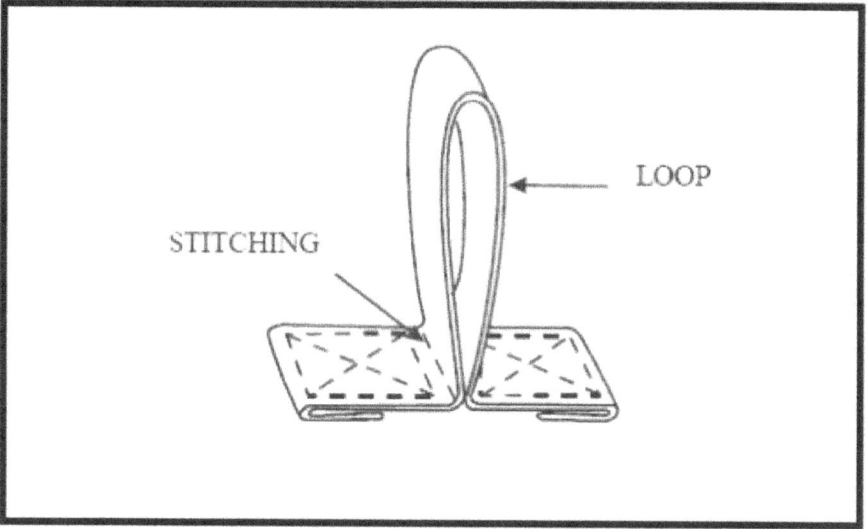

LOOP

STITCHING

Figure 13-11. Two-ply long loop

Edge-Type Loop

13-16. The edge-type loop (Figure 13-12) is used on tarpaulins for tie-line fastenings. It is also used as the female half of a toggle fastener. To make this loop

- Cut a piece of webbing twice the length of the planned loop plus enough to form a turn under at each end.
- Turn under the ends.
- Place the webbing on the canvas item so that the ends of the webbing are even and the inside edges touch.
- Sew the webbing to the canvas item with one X-shaped seam.

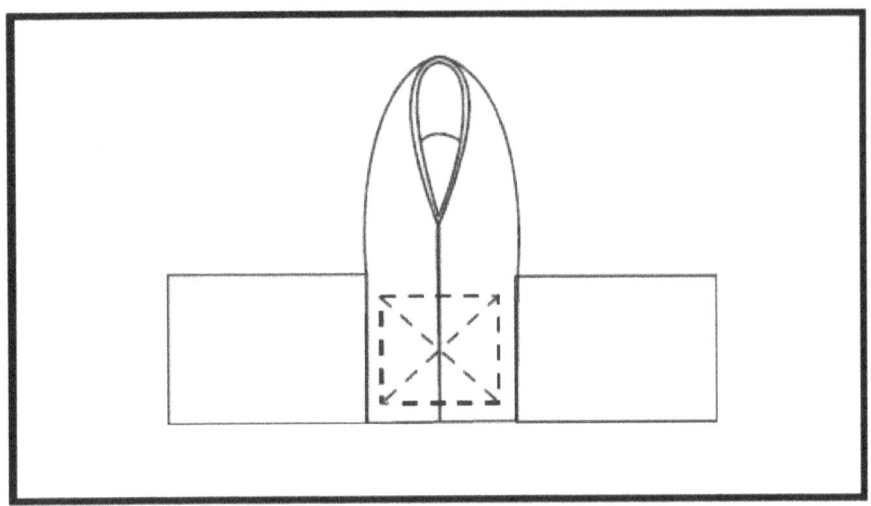

Figure 13-12. Edge-type loop

SECTION IV – Straps

13-17. Straps are bands of webbing by which canvas items are held, fastened, pulled, or lifted. The ends of straps are left plain and rolled, angled, or shaped to take hardware, billets, and chapes.

Plain-End Strap

13-18. A strap with a plain end (Figure 13-13) is a piece of webbing cut to size. The end is finished by attaching an end clip or by looping it through a piece of hardware, turning under the raw edge, and sewing it in place to the strap. A plain strap that has a buckle on one end and an end clip on the other is a billet (Figure 13-14)

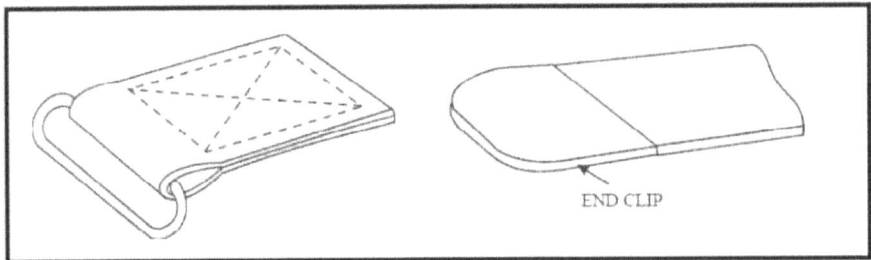

END CLIP

Figure 13-13 Plain-end strap

Rolled-End Strap

13-19. A strap with a rolled end (Figure 13-14) is tapered by rolling and folding the edges to the center of the webbing. Both the inner and outer edges are sewn in place. The end of the strap is finished by attaching an end clip, or by looping it through a piece of hardware, turning under the raw edge, and sewing it in place to the strap. If a 2 inch wide strap is tapered to a 1 inch end, the taper should be about 2 ½ inches long

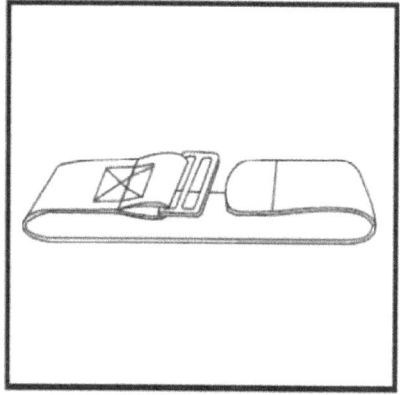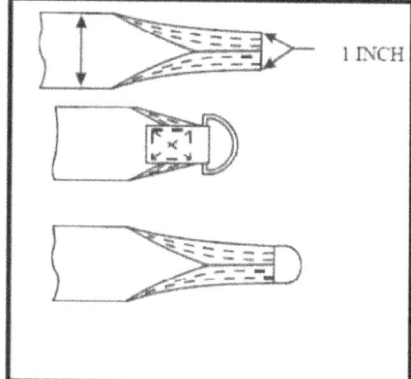

Figure 13-14. Billet and Rolled-end strap

Angled-End Strap

13-20. A strap with an angled end (Figure 13-15) has corners which have been folded to meet at the center of the strap. The strap is finished by sewing a billet on top of the angled end or by sandwiching the angled end between the two layers of a chape and sewing the chape in place

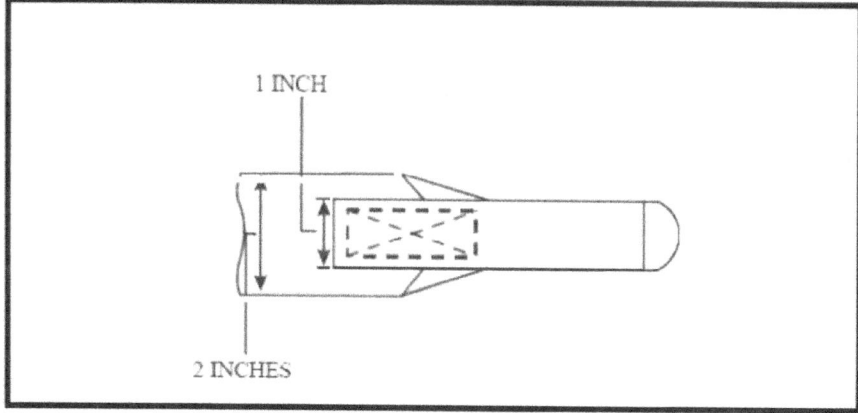

Figure 13-15. Angled-end strap

Shaped-End Strap

13-21. A strap with a shaped end (Figure 13-16) is notched, the edges are brought together, and a billet or chape is sewn in place. A piece of reinforcement webbing is usually placed under the shaped end and sewn in place when a billet is attached.

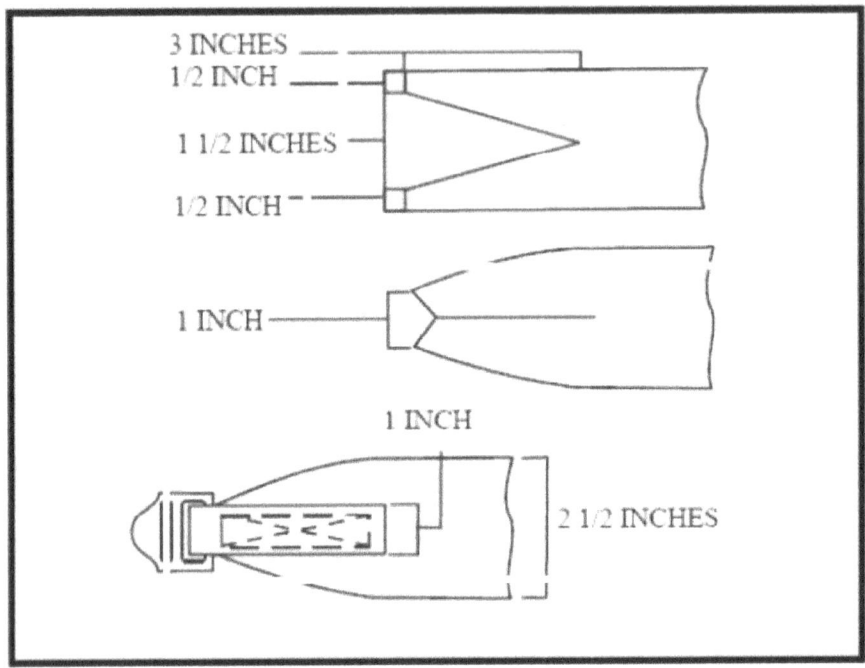

Figure 13-16. Shaped-end strap

SECTION V – Handles

13-22. Handles are pieces of webbing by which canvas items are grasped and carried. The two kinds of handles used in the repair of canvas items are plain and stitched-grip.

Plain Webbing Handle

13-23. A plain webbing handle (Figure 13-17) is used when the strain is carried along the vertical plane of the item. To make this handle

Cut a piece of webbing 12 inches long.

Position the webbing on the canvas item so that it forms an upside down U. The outside edges should be 5 ½ inches apart.

Turn under each end ½ inch.

Stitch each end of the handle in place by sewing an X-shaped seam that is about 2 inches long.

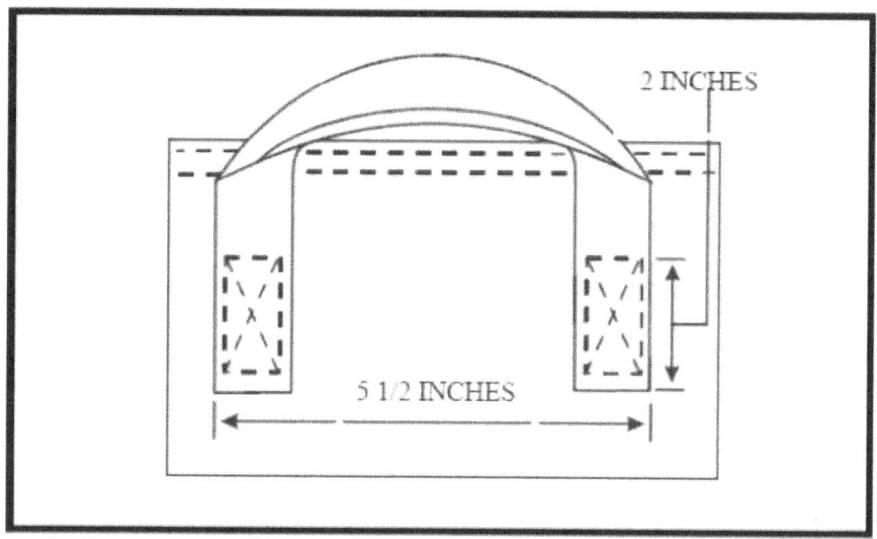

Figure 13-17. Plain webbing handle

Stitched-Grip Webbing Handle

13-24. A stitched-grip webbing handle (Figure 13-18) is used when the strain is on the horizontal plane of the item. To make this handle

- Cut a piece of 2 inch wide heavy cotton webbing 15 ¼ inches long.
- Fold the webbing in half and mark the center.
- Draw straight chalk lines across the webbing 2 ⅞ inches to the left and right sides of the center.
- Fold the edges of the webbing to the center between the lines. Taper the webbing beyond the lines.
- Stitch along the edges of the webbing between the lines. Stitch on top of each chalk line twice.
- Cut a piece of duck 5 ½ inches wide and 40 inches long to use as reinforcement backing. Turn under the raw edges ½ inch and crease the folded edges in place.
- Center the backing under the area on the canvas item where the handle will be attached.
- Stitch the backing in place.
- Turn under each end of the handle ⅝ inch.
- Center the handle on the canvas item and backing so that the ends are 12 inches apart. Leave some slack.
- Stitch the handle in place by sewing a square-shaped seam at each end.
- Cut two reinforcement pieces 4 ½ inches long from the 2 inch wide webbing.

- Center the reinforcements across the ends of the handle. Turn under the ends ½ inch and stitch them in place with X-shaped seams.

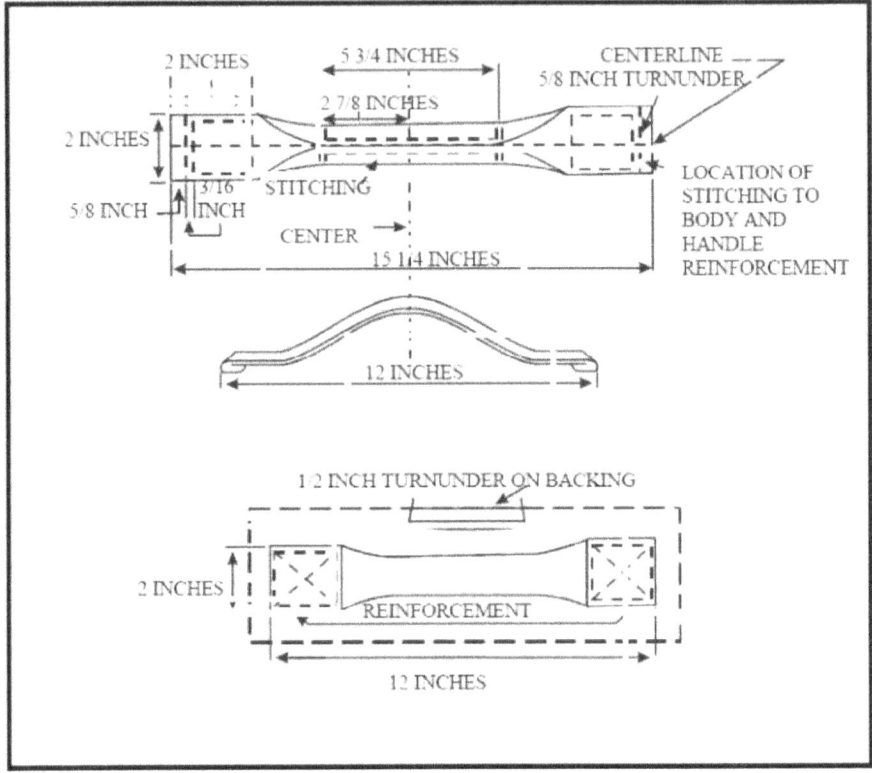

Figure 13-18. Stitched-grip webbing handle

CHAPTER 14 - RE-TREATING TENTS AND TARPAULINS

SECTION I –Re-Treating Canvas

14-1. The canvas used to make tents and tarpaulins is treated with chemicals so that it is fire-resistant, water-repellant, weather-resistant, and mildew-resistant. Exposure and cleaning decrease the chemical protection. Tents and tarpaulins should be re-treated as needed to make them more durable. To re-treat canvas—

- Re-treat tarpaulins while they are stretched out flat on the ground. Re-treat tents while they are erected or raised with a hoist. Start at the top of the tent and work down.
- Make sure the canvas is dry. Remove dirt, oil, and grease stains.
- Obtain an adequate supply of canvas preservative coating, Federal Specification TT-P-595 (NSN 8030-00-281-2346). Stir the paste thoroughly, and then dilute it with an equal amount of dry-cleaning solvent. Add the solvent a little at a time, and stir continuously until all the solvent has been added. Stir the coating again just before it is used.
- Apply the coating with a brush or spray gun. (If a spray gun is used, the operator should wear protective clothing, a respirator, and a helmet liner.
- Apply the coating more generously to patches and recently repaired areas.
- Let the canvas dry until it is thoroughly dry to the touch.

CAUTION: *While re-treating tents and tarpaulins, always apply coatings in a well ventilated area. Avoid inhalation of solvent fumes and prolonged exposure of skin to cleaning solvent. Wash exposed skin thoroughly. Dry cleaning solvent (Fed. Spec. P-D-680 and P-S-661) is potentially dangerous to personnel and property. Do not use near open flame or excessive heat.*

SECTION II – Re-Treating Seams

14-2. Seams on tents and tarpaulins require two re-treatments to prevent rot and leaks. Seams should be re-treated on a hard, flat surface. To re-treat seams on clean, dry canvas—

- Dilute the coating and use a 4 inch wide, stiff paint brush to apply one coat to the outside of every seam.
- Coat the stitching thoroughly on webbing attachments and reinforcements.
- Allow the first coat to air dry for 4 hours. (This time can be reduced by using warm air.)
- When the first coat is dry to the touch, apply a second coat.
- Allow seams to dry for at least 24 hours before erecting or repacking the tent or tarpaulin.

163

GLOSSARY

SECTION I – Acronyms & Abbreviations

AR	Army regulation
ATTN	Attention
DA	Department of Army
FM	field manual
HQ	headquarters
in	inch
MOS	military occupational specialty
NSN	national stock number
TM	technical manual
TRADOC	United States Army Training and Doctrine Command
WP	water proof

REFERENCES

SOURCES USED - These are the sources quoted or paraphrased in this publication.

Army Publications

AR 25-52, Authorized Abbreviations, Brevity Codes, and Acronyms, 4 Jan 2005.

AR 670-1, Wear and Appearance of Army Uniforms and Insignia, 3 February 2005.

PAM 25-30, Consolidated Index of Army Publications and Blank Forms, 14 July 2009.

TM 3-34.86, Rigging Techniques, Procedures, and Applications, 16 July 2012.

TM 10-227, Fitting of Army Uniforms and Footwear, 10 June 2013.

TM 10-3530-207-14, Clothing Repair Shop Trailer Mounted Model CRS-100, NSM: 3530-01-346-

7265, 28 May 1993

TM 10-8340-211-13, Operator's, Organizational, and Direct Support Maintenance Manual: Tent,

General Purpose, Small (NSN 8340-00-470-2335), Medium (NSN 83440-00-482-3962), and

Large (NSN 830-00-470-2342), 16 September 1990

TM 10-8400-201-23, Unit and Direct Support Maintenance Manual: General Repair Procedures

Clothing, 7 May 1990

Documents Needed

These documents must be available to the intended users of this publication.
8340-90-CL-PO1, Repair Kit, Tentage (NSN 8340-00-262-5767).
*AMDF, Army Master Data File.
DA Form 2028, Recommended Changes to Publications and Blank Forms.
Federal Standard 751A, Stitches, Seams, and Stitching
Available from:

> Naval Publications and Forms Center
> ATTN: NPF 105
> 5801 Tabor Avenue
> Philadelphia, PA 19120

TC 3-34.489, The Soldier and the Environment, 8 May 2001.
Unit Supply Update, Update 2-14, Unit Supply Consolidated Handbook, 28 February 1994.

*This publication is available from Commander, USAMC Catalog Data Activity, ATTN: AMXCAPP,
New Cumberland, PA 17070-5010

INDEX

TM 4-42.21
24 July 2013

By Order of the Secretary of the Army:
RAYMOND T. ODIERNO
General, United States Army
Chief of Staff

Official:
GERALD B. O'KEEFE
Acting Administrative Assistant
to the Secretary of the Army
1320405
DISTRIBUTION:
Active Army, Army National Guard, and United States Army Reserve: Not
to be distributed;
electronic media only.
PIN: 102535-000

www.ingramcontent.com/pod-product-compliance
Lightning Source LLC
Chambersburg PA
CBHW070113290526
45789CB00005B/2010